What's a
Person to Do?

What's a Person to Do?

Everyday Decisions That Matter

Mark S. Latkovic

Foreword by William E. May

Our Sunday Visitor Publishing Division
Our Sunday Visitor, Inc.
Huntington, Indiana 46750

Copyright © 2013 by Mark S. Latkovic (1963-). Published 2013.

18 17 16 15 14 13   1 2 3 4 5 6 7 8 9

ISBN: 978-1-61278-604-9 (Inventory No. T1300)
eISBN: 978-1-61278-288-1
LCCN: 2013937693

Cover design: Amanda Falk
Cover art: Thinkstock
Interior design: Dianne Nelson

PRINTED IN THE UNITED STATES OF AMERICA

For my teachers

William E. May (1928-)

and

Benedict M. Ashley, O.P. (1915-2013)

TABLE OF CONTENTS

40 Questions and Answers: Everyday Ethics in Practice

FOREWORD

By William E. May

MARK S. LATKOVIC'S *What's a Person to Do? Everyday Decisions That Matter* is a very fine introduction to the moral dimension of our lives. Latkovic, who as a good Catholic moral theologian fully accepts the God-given authority to teach on matters of faith and morals, considers only issues on which there is no authoritative magisterial teaching.

Following a "Note to the Reader," the author devotes the Introduction to an engagingly written "Ethical Toolbox" — providing tools for making good moral decisions. He shows that the "natural law" instructs us that there are some basic or fundamental human goods — life itself, including bodily life and health, knowledge of the truth and appreciation of beauty, developing and exercising our skills in work and in play, friendship and fellowship with other people, marriage and the having and raising of children — that contribute to our full flourishing as human persons. We all in some way or other realize this, and we likewise realize that it is not good freely to choose to damage, destroy, or impede these goods either in ourselves or in others. We are frequently tempted to do so — for example, to lie to others in order to get them fired so that we can have their jobs, or to kill "Ma Fia" before she kills us, or to do unto others *before they do unto us*, rather than following the Golden Rule to do unto others as we would have them do unto us. He also takes up the key roles of conscience and the moral virtues in making moral judgments.

Armed with these tools, we are ready to reflect, with Latkovic, on the questions and answers — that is, ethics in practice. He notes that many of us may not at first realize that these everyday questions involve ethics, but they do because they require us to make choices, and choices can be either good or bad — and most of us want to make true (that is, *good*) moral choices *and* carry them out. Latkovic focuses on forty everyday questions. The following are illustrative: Ought I to get cable TV and Internet access? Ought I to attend the wedding and reception of friends who cohabit (fornicate) before marriage? Ought I to give money to beggars? Ought I to tip waiters or waitresses? Ought I to use my company's printer for making copies of my personal documents? Ought I to be a "double-dipper"? Or let elderly parents drive when their driving skills are no more? Latkovic carefully examines and analyzes each of these questions, inviting the reader to think them through. He does not fear to climb out on some limbs and recognizes and invites criticism.

I highly recommend this engagingly written, mostly footnote and endnote free, introduction to everyday ethics for everyone who wants a good guide in making good moral choices.

I am very happy with this splendid work of a former student both at The Catholic University of America and at the Pontifical John Paul II Institute for Studies on Marriage and the Family, who is now a good friend and colleague.

— WILLIAM E. MAY
Emeritus Michael J. McGivney Professor of
Moral Theology, Pontifical John Paul II Institute
for Studies on Marriage and Family at
The Catholic University of America, and
Senior Research Fellow, Culture of Life Foundation

Acknowledgments

I WANT TO THANK several people: my wife and children for their patience during the writing of this book; my former teacher Dr. William E. May for reading the manuscript and writing The Foreword for the book; the staff at OSV, especially my editor Cindy Cavnar; my brother Chris Latkovic, who looked over two of the questions and offered helpful comments on them; and the staff at The Visionary, where I purchased my new pair of glasses which enabled me to finish this book, headache free.

§§§

A Note to the Reader

A User-Friendly Guide to Everyday Ethics

Have you ever had a co-worker ask you a difficult moral question that you couldn't answer? You know, one of those questions that can bug you for the rest of the day — like a movie title you can't quite recall — because you're not sure how to respond? When you get home from work, you Google the question and ... you come up empty, or at least not satisfied with what you find. If you've ever had such an experience in trying to answer a moral question, well, then this book is for you. But even if you find an answer or helpful information online that may lead you to an answer, this book may still be for you because I'm going to provide you with the ability to respond to moral conundrums from an intellectually defensible position that is in accord with sound ethics and the mind of the Church.

The moral questions that arise in everyday life are the focus of this book — the sort of questions that fall through the cracks and are overlooked or untreated in books devoted to the ethics of sex, health care, and life in society involving doctors, nurses, lawyers, politicians, businessmen, teachers, journalists, and other professionals.

These are questions of *everyday ethics* — common but difficult moral questions that most of us have encountered in some form or another but that usually don't rise to the level of national security, the taking of human life, the misuse of biotechnology, or other such serious matters. Although I cannot treat every possible question of this kind, I do hope to treat enough of them to give you, the reader, a foundation for reflecting wisely and acting uprightly when confronted with these and similar questions.

To keep this book as user-friendly as possible, I've adopted a question-and-answer format, using, for the most part, non-technical language. Before I get to those questions and their various challenges, I will offer a basic overview of ethics that provides a framework for thinking about these questions. This primer will give you a clear grasp of the steps needed to make a good moral decision and thus become a better moral person. Although this overview is geared to helping you answer the questions, it can pretty much stand on its own.

This book presupposes no prior formal training in ethics, other than the experience we all have of everyday encounters with such practical moral questions as: *What am I to do in this situation? What kind of person will I become if I do this act? What goods and bads will I bring about? How will it affect others?* Sometimes the questions that people ask — some of the very ones I present here — are not even thought to be ethical in nature; but they often are, even if it's not always obvious.

Except in a few cases, the questions raised here are also those for which the Catholic Church does not have a definitive teaching or perhaps no formal teaching at all. So this book is not focused on the "big questions" pertaining to abortion, euthanasia, stem cell research, artificial reproductive technologies, war, and capital punishment — all issues on which the Church has clearly taught and teaches in her God-given authority to teach in the name of Jesus Christ on matters of faith and morals. (For example, she teaches authoritatively on the Ten Commandments.)

But many of the book's questions are no less real or, at times, no less urgent for the individuals concerned. They don't usually make the news, but they are important. Among them are questions involving: cheating, stealing, truth-telling and lying, social justice, recycling, shopping, dating, investing, voting, tattoos, buying and selling, workplace ethics, copyright law, media usage, racial profiling, charitable giving, pets, driving, and tipping.

Ethics for Everyone

Who should read this book? Well, anyone who is concerned about coming to true moral judgments and making good moral choices should do so — namely, anyone who wants to be (more) virtuous. That should include all of us! The ethics of everyday living are for everyone. No one can avoid facing the kinds of questions I treat here, but lay people, who live in the world and often have to confront these sorts of questions, are my primary, although not my sole, target audience.

At times, I will draw from Sacred Scripture and Church teaching and tradition, but non-Catholic Christians or non-believers could benefit from both the analysis and the answers put forth here. I'll handle these questions in a way that could best be described as a *natural law approach*: one that uses human reason to seek moral truth, but a reason illuminated by Christian faith.

I'll also point out the firm dispositions to do good, called *moral virtues*, which are necessary for making good moral choices and carrying them out well. (These dispositions are either acquired by our own free choice to act in a morally good way or they are given to us by God.) Virtues such as prudence give us real insight into the best means for achieving what is truly good for us. In other words, a virtue like prudence helps us apply general principles to whatever question — in all its particularities — we face. Other virtues such as temperance (moderation) and fortitude (courage) help us to consistently carry out our choices and commitments amid difficulties, as we strive to realize human goods, while the social virtue of justice enables us to respect the legitimate rights of others.

Many of the questions we'll be grappling with come from my personal experience studying and teaching moral theology for almost thirty years. Others come from my experience as a husband and father, as well as speaking in parishes and other forums. Others come from listening to friends and family members raise issues they've struggled with and for which they have not found satisfactory answers. These are questions that are, as moral theologian Germain Grisez put it, "either widely asked, especially important, or usefully illustrative." I give it my best shot in formulating responses to them — however tentative and fallible — while avoiding, I hope, answers that may seem too lax or too strict. Moral principles and norms that the Church has articulated will also help guide us or will at least be in the background, so to speak, in the answers to many of the questions.

Each of the questions could have been worded differently and even greatly expanded, but I have tried to keep them simple and straightforward. In general, except in a few places, I have avoided dealing with questions that involve issues of cooperation — formal and material — with those doing evil. Also, in what befits a question-and-answer format, I have tried to keep my answers in a somewhat conversational style, as if we were sitting down together over a cup of coffee. And I've avoided footnotes and endnotes and referencing endless moral theology books. For the most part, any references that I do provide, especially when treating questions that involve the law, will be contained in the body of the answer.

I won't be able to say everything that could be said in response to a particular question (there are so many contingencies!), but I hope to say enough for you to begin the exciting and morally significant task of thinking through some of these questions that many have asked but for which, perhaps, they've not received an adequate answer. But first, you'll need certain tools. To help you get your footing, I've provided, next, a compact introduction to ethics designed to orient you and give you an "ethical toolbox."

INTRODUCTION

An Ethical Toolbox:
Tools for Making Good Moral Decisions

ALL OF US WANT TO MAKE GOOD MORAL DECISIONS, RIGHT? But what is involved in doing so? How do we proceed? The first thing to keep in mind is that ethics is all about the promotion and protection of basic human goods such as life, health, bodily integrity, knowledge, beauty, marriage, work, and friendship. When our actions realize goods such as these, we in turn realize more and more of our potential to flourish as human persons. But not just any realization will do, as we know all too well from experience. We have to foster these goods in ways that truly respect them for what they are: fundamental aspects of who we are as human persons who live in society with others, for "no man is an island."

Some Tools of Ethics

So, when making moral choices, we have to ask ourselves: Does this act *violate* any particular basic human good — for example, by impeding or damaging or destroying it? If it does, then I am not morally justified in doing it. For instance, the good of knowledge is surely one that is worthy to pursue. (Who, after all, is for ignorance?) But one can pursue knowledge immorally, say, by using human persons as guinea pigs or lying to gain access to a particular college course, or by experimenting on human embryos and killing them. Or one can pursue it morally by using other models for testing and experimentation, for example, or by choosing not to lie in pursuit of knowledge. An act that violates a basic good is one we should never freely choose to do, no matter what our intention or end or situation or circumstances; it is always morally bad. In the words of Catholic moral theology, it is intrinsically evil and prohibited by a moral absolute. As St. Paul teaches: We are not to do evil that good might come of it (see Romans 3:8).

Actually, most of us make decisions this way — that is, by considering their impact, either good or bad, on human goods — we're just not always aware of it! But that kind of thinking is what is going on behind the scene when we make a moral decision, whether good or bad. Those of us who were raised as Christians probably have used the Ten Commandments as our guide to morally good living (see Exodus 20:2-17; Deuteronomy 5:6-21). We have also looked to the lives of the saints and to our parents as guides in the formation of moral virtue. How tragic are the lives of children whose parents failed to teach them to respect others and to love their neighbors as themselves. What better way to learn ethics than by observing virtuous people!

We have also, I am sure, relied on the Golden Rule — a principle that is attributed to Jesus when he said, "Do to others whatever you would have them do to you. This is the law and the prophets" (Matthew 7:12). But it's also common to many ethical systems besides Christianity. We will rely on the Golden Rule often in this book. It does not mean, as the old adage has it, "He who has the gold, rules"! Rather, as St. Thomas Aquinas reasons, it makes more specific or concrete the master moral principle of love of neighbor as oneself: I should treat others as I would want them to treat me.

This "tight relation between the love principle and the Golden Rule," writes John Finnis, Catholic moral philosopher and legal scholar, "suggests that love and justice, though analytically distinguishable, certainly cannot be contrasted as other and other. 'Neighbor' excludes no human being anywhere, insofar as anyone could be benefited by one's choices and actions. To love some-

one is essentially to will that person's good" (http://plato.stanford
.edu/entries/aquinas-moral-political/#SupMorPri).

Catholics speak of another important guide to the ethics of
everyday living: the Magisterium, or the teaching authority of the
Church composed of the pope and the bishops. When Catholics
go about forming their conscience, Church teaching should be
uppermost in their minds. They need to ask: *What* and *how* does
the Church teach on this matter? And *why* does she teach what
she teaches? In listening to the Magisterium, Catholics are really
listening to Christ (see Luke 10:16).

Conscience: Conventional or Catholic?

But what about *conscience,* you ask? We often hear that following our conscience is what's most important. Is that true? The
short answer is yes. But in our secular culture today, there are
many spurious notions of conscience, such as Freud's "superego,"
or the reigning current opinion as manifested in such things as
Gallup polls, or what one "feels" is right and just. This notion of
conscience is foreign to the one we find in the Bible and Church
teaching. It is subjective and looks much like a mirror of the culture — call it "conventional" conscience. And there is great pressure in our fallen world to conform to it rather than to Christ.
But our conscience must be fully *conformed to Christ* and to what
is truly good for us before we can follow it. In a word, it must be
carefully *formed.*

A Catholic conscience looks very different from the prevail-
ing secular notion. Conscience isn't about doing what we feel like
doing or doing what the culture tells us to do, but rather our
awareness of moral truth. St. Paul tells us that God has "written"
his law on our hearts (see Romans 2:14-15). Conscience is our
understanding of this law of God, which tells us to do this or not
to do that. We can also speak of this law on the heart as the *natu-*

ral moral law: that law which the human mind can know apart from divine revelation, but which, on account of sin and human fallibility, God revealed to us for our benefit.

Reading the *Catechism of the Catholic Church* (CCC); consulting a trusted, knowledgeable, and faithful priest; gathering all the facts; studying how the relevant moral principles apply to the case at hand; and praying to the Holy Spirit for wisdom are some of the key steps in forming your conscience. In attempting to answer the questions in this book — or any ethical questions — we are engaged, whether we know it or not, in the task of conscience formation. That is, we are searching for moral *truth*, searching for what we ought to do because it's the right thing to do — not because it's necessarily the easiest, the most popular, or the one that promises the best consequences for the majority of people. Consequences are important, of course, but they're not the most important aspect of the ethical decision for the moral agent.

The purpose of conscience is to give us our *last best judgment* about this act's moral goodness or badness. Knowingly to act against our conscience, then, is to act immorally. That's why we're obliged to heed its voice when, and only when, it's well formed. You see, conscience tells us that this act being considered is something that I should or should not do, that it is something either in conformity with God's law or not. And if conscience is our last best judgment here and now about what we are to do, then it must be rooted in basic principles of morality such as those excluding the free choice to damage, destroy, or impede a basic human good either in ourselves or in others.

Conscience might say the following at the moment of choice: there is a moral norm against doing this deed — for example, "You shall not lie," which is an *absolute* norm. If I do it, I will make myself to *be* a liar. (Of course, defining *what* a lie is can be difficult at times.) This happens because my free choices to do either good or evil profoundly shape and form me, making me to *be* the person that I am with *this* particular moral character, with *this* particular moral identity. By their fruits you shall know them, Jesus proclaims (see Matthew 7:16).

Whether we realize it or not, each of us, through our free choices, is becoming either a sinner or a saint, either hideous or holy. Answering questions such as the ones in this book well is part and parcel of our effort to grow in the image of God that we already are (see Genesis 1:26-27). In sum, it is the effort to root out personal sin — both mortal and venial — in our lives and grow in holiness. And that's what saints, future dwellers of the Kingdom, are all about.

Ethics and Happiness

Speaking of the saints, let me add a final word about the nature of ethics, but one now explicitly illuminated by faith. What we can call a *faith ethic* is all about attaining true human happiness, not just observing what some see as a collection of mere rules, of do's and don'ts. But the saints know that this authentic happiness is found only in *holiness*, only in doing what the Lord wants us to do. Our vocation is to be holy as our heavenly Father is holy. We are called to be saints. There really is a profound connection between sanctity and happiness.

In the Beatitudes of his Sermon on the Mount, Jesus answers the question that each of us has asked deep down: *How do I achieve happiness?* Our Lord shows us that happiness is achieved not in status or in wealth, not in pleasure or in possessions, but in doing the will of the Father (see Matthew 4:3-10). This is how we become perfect as he is perfect (see Matthew 5:48).

Each of the Beatitudes, as St. Augustine saw many centuries ago, is a Christian virtue that leads us from humility to wisdom to happiness. "Blessed are the poor in spirit"; "Blessed are the pure in heart"; "Blessed are those who are persecuted for righteousness' sake" (Matthew 5:3, 8, 10; RSV). These are among the keys to a lasting and legitimate happiness — imperfect now (as our sins and sufferings make evident!), but perfect in God's kingdom.

Before a Christian acts, he or she should ask over and above the natural law: *How does this act affect my relationship with Christ? Does it violate one of these Christian virtues, one of Christ's Beatitudes?* The Beatitudes are not pious phrases, but normative guidelines for Christian living and loving. They enable us, with God's grace, to do what is pleasing to him. Our answers to the questions here will benefit from listening to what the Beatitudes tell us about ethical choices.

The Beatitudes — and the gifts of the Holy Spirit, such as wisdom and understanding — do not eliminate our need for the Ten Commandments and the moral virtues but rather, as they build on them, they empower us to live a good moral life according to Christ's new commandment, his Law of Love: "Love one another. As I have loved you, so you also should love one another" (John 13:34). Without the Commandments, and the moral virtues to strengthen and support us, we could not live a moral life in Christ in the power of the Spirit. They lay the foundation for our freedom to choose what is morally good according to what is reasonable.

The Beatitudes and gifts, on the other hand, enable us to live a moral life directed by the promptings of the Holy Spirit. The Ten Commandments and the Beatitudes are not contrary to each other, but rather complementary, as Blessed Pope John Paul II noted in his great 1993 encyclical on the moral life, *The Splendor of Truth* (n. 16). Thus, we need both to be both morally good people and godly people.

With our ethical toolkit in hand — and with the help of many other ethical principles, virtues, and moral norms scattered throughout the book — we can begin answering our questions.

40

QUESTIONS AND ANSWERS:

EVERYDAY ETHICS IN PRACTICE

1.
Should our family have cable TV and Internet access in our home?

This is one of those "Are you kidding me?" questions. I bet that most people wouldn't give this question a second thought. Doesn't everyone have access to these services in their homes? Aren't they considered basic necessities in today's society? So is this really a moral question?

Of course, cable TV and the Internet are an important part of our ability to function in the modern world. They give us access to goods, such as knowledge, that are real and valuable. But we all know as well that there's morally objectionable material that we can easily access with these technologies. We know, too, that we can become addicted to watching TV and surfing the Web. We're also aware that the time we spend online and viewing all these cable channels might be better spent doing some other worthwhile activity. So, yes, this is a question that *is* morally significant.

The question really hit home for me one late summer night in 2011 when I was channel surfing after we had switched our service to a well-known cable company. As I clicked the remote, expecting to see our basic cable stations, I encountered very explicit pornography — not just on one channel but on several. The next morning, my wife called the cable company to complain and to have them delete the porn channels. It turns out that the cable box we were given so that we would have access to the programming guide was not re-programmed or "wiped clean" from the last customer — an error they said that happens, but not often. The unsuspecting Latkovic family had gotten a box loaded with the offending channels. I shudder to think that it could have been my then pre-teen daughter or three teenagers mistakenly stumbling onto those channels.

Now, I do not like the idea of my money going to support companies that provide morally objectionably fare, even while they offer me almost limitless valuable information. That said, I do not think that it is always immoral ("intrinsically evil") to subscribe to cable and Internet services through companies such as Comcast. First, however, I think that families have an obligation to search for companies that do not, as a matter of policy, offer pornography. Second, if that is not a realistic option, then families with children need to be very cautious in making sure that parental controls are put in place. Third, families should also avoid subscribing — or think about unsubscribing, if they already have access — to channels that, while they do not offer pornography, do offer material that is often both extremely violent and sexually explicit. One way to do this might be to pay simply for a basic cable package that does not include such channels as HBO, which offer more explicit fare including pornography.

A sound guide to follow in regard to media viewing, one stringently followed by a bishop friend of mine, is the old saying, "Don't tempt your virtue." In other words, make sure you have the television and computer in a well-traveled location in the home, that you lay down very clear and consistent rules about what sites and channels can be viewed, and that you provide one-on-one guidance for young children and teens in the home, preferably being around when they are watching TV or on the computer.

As we think about this question, the best approach is twofold. First, we must realize our need to acquire the virtue of *moderation* so that we can properly limit our TV viewing and electronic gadget use. The virtue of moderation will also prevent us from succumbing to the temptation to sins of lust and unreasonable anger in the things that we are exposed to in the media. It can also help us with other addictive gadgets such as the iPhone, iPod, Blackberry, Nook, Tablet, and Kindle. People used to call the Blackberry a "Crackberry" to indicate its addictive quality!

Second, we must approach the question from the perspective of how we can best witness to the world and to our families the truth that *Jesus is Lord*. Here we arrive back at moral conscience. If we believe that bringing these services into our homes goes against our conscience because we see it as contrary to that witness, then we should not do so. But we can also believe otherwise with a clear conscience. We just need to speak a little louder to let the cable companies know that we don't appreciate all of their morally lousy channels and programming.

Clearly, we are cooperating with the cable company in giving them our money in return for a service. I would say, however, that this cooperation is of the kind that can be justified in most circumstances. In the language of traditional moral theology, the cooperation is of the remote (or distant) mediate material kind for an individual or family who in no way intends the evils of pornography (or watches it) but simply wills the good things that the cable subscription provides. It is not "formal cooperation," which is always wrong. But subscribers must do all they can to mitigate any bad side effects of having cable in the home.

This question receives its moral aspect because of the goods of human life and sexuality that we need to protect from harm, in this case by observing the Fifth, Sixth, and Ninth Commandments. The Beatitudes, too, speak about how blessed are "the pure of heart" and blessed are "the meek." We want to have pure hearts and pure homes. However *you* answer the question, make sure you steadfastly guard that purity, in yourselves and your children.

One practical suggestion: Some families with pre-adolescent children do not permit use of TV in their homes. Rather, they show the children good material that is available on DVDs, many developed by such sources at EWTN (the Eternal Word Television Network), Ignatius Press, and other reliable Catholic media.

§§§

2.

Should I feel responsible to give money to homeless people begging on the street?

Okay, so now you say, "Here's a question I can relate to!" Who hasn't been approached by beggars — often homeless people — asking for money? Many of us hesitate to give money to them out of fear of being harmed or scammed, but then afterward we feel guilty for having ignored them. Many of these individuals seem to be in dire straits for one reason or another, often because of alcohol, drugs, or mental illness. Even if we would like to help them, we must ask if it's prudent to do so. Indeed, we don't want to make things worse for them if, after giving them money, they use it to buy alcohol or it's stolen from them.

At the same time, we may be familiar with the prophet Isaiah's imperative about giving shelter to the homeless (see Isaiah 58:7). Nonetheless, it might be wiser to help these people in a way that does not involve giving them money, at least not directly. For example, it might be better to help the homeless by buying them a meal or providing them with temporary shelter, if that is possible and if we can do so safely. Many parishes run a warming center for the homeless in the winter where they can get a hot meal and a hot shower. Having helped out with this program myself, I can testify to its worthiness. In general, we may also support homeless shelters with our time and talents, especially if we find ourselves called to do so.

Christian compassion tells us that we must help these unfortunate souls, but in a way that's truly going to make a difference in their lives and not just soothe our conscience. This would involve some of us working with mental health professionals and others to provide direct help. After the homeless were deinstitutionalized many years ago, the funding for mental health services that was supposed to have helped these people never materialized. Often the homeless have families, so it's not always a problem of finding shelter but of their mental illness and alcohol and drug abuse which keeps them on the street by "choice."

§§§

3.
Should I laugh at a dirty joke?

Well, I don't want to sound like former President Bill Clinton who engaged in some creative word parsing during his impeachment ordeal, but I do think it all depends on what we mean by "dirty." Clearly, jokes that rely on racism, blasphemy, or other forms of harm to people are morally inappropriate (for example, a joke that is made at another's expense — and sometimes practical jokes fall into this category — hurting that person's feelings). Yet often one man's "harmless" dirty joke is another man's sinful speech. I would give you some examples, but it's better if I refrain!

It's probably safe to say that there are various levels of dirtiness involved here, ranging from an off-color joke to one that is quite raunchy and vile. We even know this to be true with certain comedians who range on a scale of clean to dirty, with various levels of offensiveness in between. Often in this area we find ourselves relying on the old standby — the *yuck* factor: that is, how I *feel* after I hear it. Do I want to shower after I hear it? Other versions of it go something like this: As with pornography, "you'll know it when you see it — or hear it." In other words, you'll know whether it's morally appropriate to laugh or not when you hear it.

Much depends, I believe, on who's telling the joke, when and where it's told, for what purpose, whether scandal will be caused in the telling (for example, will the listener be led into sin?), and so forth. The virtue of temperance helps us to know when a joke is not to be laughed at but rather scorned. So, there is no moral absolute against such a joke.

Still, isn't it a much better Christian witness to the good of speech if our tongues speak only what is good and pure, only what uplifts and inspires, avoiding not only cursing and swearing but also foul and lewd talk? There is enough crudeness in our world today without our contributing more to it. St. Paul tells us to rid ourselves of "obscene language" (Colossians 3:8; other translations speak of "filthy language"). Might he have had in mind the dirty jokes of his day?

Of course, you may hurt the jokester's feelings if you don't laugh, so it might be more charitable to explain why you're not. That may even be a powerful faith witness. It may also be an effective way to remove these sorts of jokes from our everyday life.

§§§

4.
Can I read a book or attend a play or
watch a movie with risqué parts?

Get ready for a long answer. Some of you have heard of the erotic
trilogy (I hate to use the term *book*), *Fifty Shades of Grey*. It's a
best-seller and especially popular with women. Unfortunately, it's
also a book that features graphic portrayals of kinky sex, including
sadism, masochism, and bondage. Reading a book of this kind
poses a real moral question, even if in the minds of some people
the trilogy is not technically pornographic since it features no pic-
tures (although I'm sure a movie is in the works). I could write
a whole book about this question, but I'll try to condense my
answer to a bite-sized portion.

A few years ago I had to confront this question head-on when
my teenage son was required to read Ken Kesey's *One Flew Over
the Cuckoo's Nest* for his sophomore English class. I remembered
reading the book as a high school student in the late 1970s and
knew that it contained many scenes of explicit sex, foul language,
and violence. My wife and I objected and told the school authorities at our son's Catholic co-ed school that he should not
be required to read such a book at his age, fifteen. We eventually
reached a satisfactory accommodation, but I won't bore you with
the details of that.

Though both his school and mine were Catholic schools
— and the book, it's safe to say, contradicted the values taught
there, and in the home, and at church — the usual outside pres-
sures played into assigning it. Sure, that contradiction of values
is going to happen in many academic disciplines, either because
of the teacher's views or because of the subject matter itself, but
the child's age, level of maturity, and so forth must be taken into
account in determining what is and is not appropriate for the
student, whether in elementary school or high school. It's true

we cannot shelter our children, but parents should make the call regarding such delicate subjects as sex and violence, and decide what's best or suitable for their own offspring.

For adults, there might be many legitimate reasons why reading a book with explicit sexual themes may be perfectly moral, as well as necessary. Sometimes, for example, parents need to familiarize themselves with the literature their children are reading in school. Educators may have to read books that feature extreme sex and violence as plot themes as part of their teaching profession. Those who work in the fields of sexual ethics or chastity education and similar professions and ministries need to be informed about what adults and teens are exposed to in the secular culture of movies, music, and magazines. Sometimes this can and should be done simply by reading or listening to the reviews of those whose opinion one trusts. They get paid to provide this information!

When the necessary precautions are taken, reading or reviewing novels and other books with sexually themed plots that are very explicit may not only be right, but part of one's duty or vocation as teacher, educator, parent, book or movie reviewer, journalist, and so on. If, however, you struggle with a sex addiction or are easily tempted with sins of lust (and who does not struggle with lust at times?), it might not be at all wise to read or watch sexually charged "artistic expressions" that could really just be soft-core porn. There is a big difference between porn (soft or hardcore) and art!

Your primary motivation in reading or watching such works should not be to be *entertained* (though that may well happen unintentionally) but to gain *knowledge* so that you can help those you serve (your students or children or audience of readers or listeners) to understand and critique the specific work in question.

But what if you don't have these educative purposes in mind when considering reading these kinds of books? What if you want to read *Fifty Shades of Grey* or see *Magic Mike*, the movie about male strippers, simply to be entertained? What if you want to listen to rap music that is filled with sexually obscene lyrics, maybe to liven up a party? Or how about watching a movie with large amounts of gratuitous violence and sex, plus lots of f-bombs? (Sounds like we might be talking about Al Pacino's movie *Scarface*.)

First, we need to emphasize that both play and aesthetic experience are truly fundamental goods of human existence and necessary for human beings and their full flourishing. Playing games (including exciting video games!), reading literature, attending the theater, listening to music, and so forth are all good and necessary components of a complete human life, when done properly with respect for the same moral norms and moral principles that govern all human activity (see the Introduction to this book). Just because we are in the realm of entertainment — broadly defined to include both high and low culture — doesn't mean that we are now also in a moral-free zone of behavior where we can do whatever we want. And yes, sorry, that includes our favorite rock bands and rock music of all types.

All forms of entertainment should attempt to uplift the human spirit, not degrade it or bring it down, even when dealing with sensitive and controversial material, such as the Holocaust and portraying vividly the terrible violence that took place. I think in this regard of Steven Spielberg's multiple-Oscar-winning film *Schindler's List*, released in 1993 (although, at the time, the film was criticized for being exploitive of Jewish suffering). Just because a movie treats a sad or serious subject does not mean that it cannot uplift and even entertain at the same time.

And it makes sense to say that works of art — including the music, novels, paintings, and movies of popular culture — that are morally and aesthetically ennobling would contribute to the ennobling and development of the human person, whereas works whose primary purpose is to titillate, to shock, and to sexually arouse would not achieve these goals, would not ennoble and develop the human person. As the saying goes, "Garbage in, garbage out."

But how, you might ask, do you determine when, say, a book or movie is simply trash? Well, first you should ask: What is the nature of this book or movie? Is its overriding theme sexually prurient in nature? That is, is the book's *predominant end* or *chief purpose* to serve as fuel for sexual fantasies and thus merely to sexually arouse? Or does the book or movie have a more serious message to communicate, even though it may present its message in a mixed sort of way — that is, using sex and violence as an integral element of the plot? Not gratuitously, mind you, but rather instrumentally to further the plot along and express its meaning and message more authentically and realistically.

You may remember the famous topless scene between the prostitute and the Holocaust survivor played by actor Rod Steiger in the critically acclaimed 1964 movie *The Pawnbroker*. This is, to me, an example of the kind of ethically sound depiction of onscreen sexuality: its purpose is not in any way to "turn on" the audience, but to make a point integral to the plot. In fact, no sexual activity takes place at all in the scene. (*The Pawnbroker* was one of the first American films to include nudity — and then, unfortunately, the floodgates opened with nudity often depicted not artistically, but pornographically.) The question that needs to be asked, though, is this: Could the scene have been shot just as effectively without the partial nudity? Maybe, maybe not. We can have a legitimate disagreement on this question.

There are lots of books out there that are both good literature and good entertainment. Christians especially should be aware of the dangers of consuming entertainment of any kind that contains images and messages contrary to the Gospel of Jesus — whether it has sex or violence or not. (And yes, I'm aware that the Bible portrays sex and violence too, but don't compare that to today's pornography!) Much as we saw with question three, Christians must be on guard against reading and watching anything that can harm their soul. Much of TV these days is littered with shows that fall into this category of harmful, despite the fact that there are many good programs as well, programs that teach or inform or entertain.

This doesn't mean, as noted, that Christians should not enjoy themselves and have fun through various forms of art. Nor does it mean that they should worry incessantly to the point of scrupulosity over these matters. But as with many of our other questions, the virtues of prudence, temperance, and fortitude are required to help ensure that our reading, watching, and listening are morally good. *Prudence* is required so that we might have the wisdom to make good choices regarding what we read, watch, listen to, and so forth — in other words, that we know the difference between good art and bad art. *Fortitude*, that we might have the courage and backbone — in spite of peer pressure and our own desire — to refuse to join the crowd to read, watch, and listen to trashy entertainment. And *temperance* and *chastity*, to help us control our thoughts, emotions, feelings, and fantasies — whether of anger or sex — when because of our vocation or profession, it's necessary for us to read and watch forms of artistic expression that may not be morally upright.

At the end of the day, we have to ask ourselves what kind of culture we want for ourselves, our children, and our grandchildren. Is it a culture of violence and eroticism or one of true love and nonviolence, after the example of Christ's Beatitudes, especially those concerning purity of heart and meekness? We have to ask ourselves further if we are setting the best possible example for others or possibly scandalizing them in our choice of entertainment. Christians are called to be different in regard to their choices.

One parting thought: It is also a good idea to pray to the Holy Spirit for the necessary guidance and strength when it behooves you for a good reason to read a novel, watch a movie or TV show, or listen to a piece of music that is morally problematic. We are, for weal or woe, affected by what we take in from the culture. To say we're not affected is to profoundly deceive ourselves.

§§§

5.
Am I under any kind of moral obligation
to avoid littering and to recycle products?

The short answer to this one is yes, especially when it involves the possibility of reusing a particular product rather than simply throwing it in the garbage. The long answer is more complicated. Although questions have been raised about the cost and energy involved in the process of recycling certain products, on balance I think that in the case of many products it is much better to recycle them than not to. It also seems wise to try to buy products whose packaging is made of biodegradable material. The facts seem to indicate that our landfills are, well, filling up. Because our natural environment is a gift from God that we have been given *steward-ship* over, we have a moral responsibility to exercise our dominion over creation with care and moderation (see Genesis 1:26, 28; CCC 2415). In other words, dominion doesn't mean domination.

Recycling does not appear to be such a burden that it would take us away from other pressing matters and thus would impose no positive duty on us at all. We need to have a greater awareness of how we treat the garden we call Earth that God has given humanity, not only to consume but also, since many natural resources are finite, to conserve for present and future generations. It is true that human invention and ingenuity, when harnessed to technology, can often overcome various limits to growth and even scarcity itself, but that doesn't mean that we should waste those resources that are limited — at least limited as far as we know.

The way I see it, we have a civic and a moral duty not to litter, as well as a moral duty to recycle. Recycling is not an absolute duty, but when we can do it, we should. The circumstances helping one judge that a sound positive norm to recycle is not binding may have to do with whether your community has a recycling program (most cities do) or whether for some reason you are not able to recycle because you judge that recycling would be more costly to you than not recycling — if, for example, you have to drive many miles to the nearest recycling plant because your city does not have curbside pickup.

Finally, there is also an aesthetic aspect to our moral duties to recycle and avoid littering: the litter and garbage we see all around us is truly ugly. As the British author and psychiatrist Theodore Dalrymple observes, not only is there a moral dimension to littering, but our litter and garbage reveal much about us today — and it's not very good. From gum left on sidewalks to glass scattered on beaches, we seem to be very careless with what we do with our garbage. And it should go without saying that carelessness could also lead to dangerous situations for motorists and pedestrians alike, especially when large objects are discarded in the road.

Recycling can contribute to the restoration of beauty in our neighborhoods and cities. As I am out walking in my neighborhood, I sometimes find myself asking, "Why is that product in the garbage? Why wasn't it recycled, donated to a needy person, or simply fixed?" Or, seeing the massive amounts of litter everywhere, I ask, "How did that trash end up on the street?" These are the kinds of questions we all have to ask ourselves — and then maybe we have to pick up the empty wrappers, cigarette butts, and plastic water bottles as we make our way over to scrub the park walls clean of graffiti.

If we can't expect people to recycle and keep their neighborhoods litter-free, how can we expect them to initiate the kinds of radical changes in their own lives some say are needed to fight the phenomenon of global warming/climate change?

§§§

6.
Do I have a moral obligation to reveal all of my house's flaws to an interested buyer?

Many years ago, when my wife and I bought our first home, we had it inspected and also asked the owners if there had been any water in the basement. No, they told us, there had not been a problem with any flooding whatsoever. Well, eventually, water came into our basement after heavy rains, and it appeared that there had been a history of water seeping into the basement before we bought the home. Needless to say, we felt a bit burned. This wasn't an inexpensive purchase with a minor flaw — no, it was an expensive purchase with a major flaw.

Given this negative experience of house buying, I think that the best way to arrive at an answer is to invoke the Golden Rule. The sellers must ask themselves: "How do I want to be treated when I go to buy a house? Would I consider it fair for the home-owner to knowingly withhold significant information about the house that could influence my decision to purchase the home?"

Of course, you may feel pressure to sell your home and thus hesitate to reveal problems to your realtor and potential buyers that could hinder a sale. In our case, when we went to sell our home twelve years later during the Great Recession (2007-2009), the city inspector told us of a number of items that needed fixing to bring the house up to code before we could put it on the market. But we had every intention anyway of making known all the defects of our home that we were aware of, at least those that any reasonable person would want to know about, such as water in the basement, structural problems, roof damage, and so on. Hence, we're talking about defects that are serious — ones that could deter a homebuyer — not squeaky doors and sticking light switches. And we also felt an obligation, if need be, to make known any problems with neighbors (this should always be disclosed) and the neighborhood at the time (there were no major ones) that would have been relevant to the sale of our home. Obviously, you are not in a position to reveal information that may come to light in the future, information that you could not reasonably have been expected to know.

Philosopher and author Thomas L. Carson makes useful distinctions between lying, deception, withholding information, and concealing information. Only the first — lying — is always morally wrong. And while the second, deception, is usually wrong, it need not be. The last two may or may not be wrong; much depends on the intent, the end, and the context. For example, if it's a case of the Gestapo at my door looking for Jews, I need not reveal any information at all, and in fact, may conceal it by some means (for example, by ambiguous speech) when they ask if I am hiding any Jews. Although many would argue that I may not lie in this situation, I am under no moral obligation to *reveal* the truth. (This is part of what's called the strategy of "mental reservation," and it was often used licitly and illicitly in these kinds of difficult situations, as well as more common day-to-day situations. It does not always involve lying, although it may.)

If I am selling my house, then I am not to lie, to deceive, or to withhold or conceal information that a buyer needs in order to make a reasonably informed decision. This does not mean that the onus is only on the seller. The buyer has the responsibility to inspect the home thoroughly and to ask questions that will elicit information that maybe the seller has forgotten or does not even think is relevant but might be relevant to the buyer.

Although what one is morally required to reveal is not the same as what one is legally required to reveal, there is much overlap, even if the former goes beyond the latter. Here's some useful information from the Internet and a good summary of the issue of disclosure as it pertains to selling a home:

[I]n recent years, the general trend towards consumer protection has included a change in the laws of most states on what needs to be disclosed. In most states, if you're selling a home it is [unlike in the past] illegal to fail to disclose major physical defects in your property, such as a basement that floods in heavy rains. You may need to make written disclosures to indicate what you know about the condition of your home. In some states, seller disclosures are still voluntary, but even then you may want to consider telling the buyer what you know. A major cause of post-sale disputes and lawsuits is defects and disclosure, and most disputes can be avoided if proper disclosures are made. This is an area of the law that changes rapidly, differs widely from state to state, and may be affected by local ordinances, so consult your lawyer for up-to-date information on the law that applies to you. ("What to Disclose When Selling a Home," http://www.moneylawoffices .com/WHAT%20TO%20DISCLOSE%20WHEN%20 SELLING%20A%20HOME.htm)

We eventually sold our home some nine months later and, like most, at quite a loss, yet grateful that we sold it in such a bad economy. But taking a large hit was common then during the Great Recession, as it is now, in a housing market that has been greatly depressed for so long, even if it shows some signs of recovery. Nonetheless, truth-telling and honesty in business dealings are the duty of every buyer and seller even if what constitutes honesty may often be hard to come by and hard to act on in a complicated economy that often behaves like a roller coaster.

§§§

7.

Should my wife and I tell our kids
the truth about Santa Claus' existence?

Spoiler alert on this one: I may be receiving some angry letters from readers because of the answer I'm about to give! If you're a parent like me, I'm sure that you have been faced with this question. I must admit that my wife and I went along with the standard approach: We told our four children that Santa Claus exists, and they went on believing so until they got older and wised up. When they would ask point-blank if Santa Claus exists, we would find ourselves mumbling something — usually softly — that didn't really make a lot of sense. In our case, however, we were always very clear in trying to connect Santa Claus with the historical figure of St. Nicholas, a fourth-century bishop in Turkey, who was the original model for Santa Claus.

At this point you may be asking yourself, "What is the harm in letting kids believe in Santa? Why make a big deal over it and be a killjoy?" My concern is this: If we hide the truth from our children about Santa Claus, then we place a level of mistrust in them that may be hard to overcome when we're talking to them about God and matters of the faith, with the expectation that they truly believe what we say. Whether we actually foster this mistrust in them does not allow us to avoid the plain truth that we usually have to tell our kids lies, albeit small ones, to keep the secular Santa myth alive.

Of course, if your children are the only ones who are in on the secret, that might cause some problems with their friends and the parents of these friends if your kids reveal the secret. But you can communicate to your children the truth that the Santa Claus of the mall and movies is really a representation or symbol of the original — that is, St. Nick. Now of course this does not mean that you have to reveal this information in full; much depends upon the child's age and level of maturity. It is often better to wait and let them ask you the question before addressing the issue. But the good of religious and moral truth is much too precious to risk squandering with a falsehood, even if it can be argued that it is a small lie and everyone's perpetuating it.

I should point out that I'm not the only one taking this approach to Santa Claus. The esteemed contemporary philosopher Edward Feser does too.

§§§

8.

Is it morally problematic for my teenage daughter to shop at Victoria's Secret?

If you have daughters, you very well might find yourself confronting this question. And if you have confronted it? Well, right now you may be exclaiming, "Uh oh!" In my experience, most people don't give much thought to where they shop as long as the prices are right and the service is good. But whether it's our daughters or our sons, the question not only of *what* we spend money on but *where* we spend it is morally significant.

Victoria's Secret and other stores that are devoted largely to selling merchandise that is overtly sexual in nature should not be supported in any way — whether buying from them or working for them or investing in them. Victoria's Secret sells very revealing lingerie, bathing suits, and other provocative clothing. And it doesn't matter whether you're a married or unmarried customer; they welcome your dollars regardless. Clearly, they're not in the business of promoting modesty or marriage to say the least. Their catalogue is really soft-core porn. Their television and billboard advertisements are as well.

Companies such as Victoria's Secret contribute directly to the sexualization of the culture, and they play a role in leading men to view our wives, daughters, and sisters as sex objects.

Clothing should protect our bodies properly, but it should also guard the sexual values of the person so that people of the opposite sex are not tempted to sins of immoderate sexual pleasure. Yet often today we see even pre-teen girls wearing skimpy bikinis, an item of clothing inappropriate for young and old alike. Clothing has a very legitimate role in contributing to the inner and outer beauty of the person, but in my opinion Victoria's Secret's merchandise mostly does just the opposite.

Most important, have a friendly conversation with your daughter (or son) about why Victoria's Secret and stores that sell similar items or worse are not to be patronized. This conversation should include a discussion of modesty (a certain reserve or moderation in dress, behavior, and speech), chastity (sexual expression that is in accord with our state in life, as either in the married, priestly, religious, or single life), and how the various types of "sex stores" do great harm to the development and stability of these virtues. Indeed, they directly contribute to a culture that is already consumed with and confused over sex.

§§§

9.
Are ethical issues involved in deciding whether and when to let our child have a cell phone?

On this matter, I think much depends on the maturity of the child and the reason(s) for providing him or her with the cell phone. As with all technology, whether it be a smart phone, an iPod, or a video game, its use can become in some way addictive for the user due to the pleasure its use provides. Thus, the virtue of moderation is especially needed when the questions concern right use, pleasure, and the potential harm (as well as the potential benefit) to important human goods associated with a particular technology.

Our youngest child received her first cell phone just before she turned thirteen, while our older three children received theirs around the ages of fourteen and fifteen. Some parents allow their children to have one a bit younger than the age at which our youngest received hers, a variation that seems appropriate. As with our previous questions, there are for the most part no hard-and-fast rules that apply here. But there are some significant prudential and moral guidelines that can be offered to help ensure that the cell phone will not become a problem, as when it is used for "sexting" or stalking or bullying.

In general, parents need to make it clear that the child does not have a right to a cell phone. It is a privilege that can be taken away. Establishing very clear rules regarding how the phone is to be used falls within the parents' responsibility and right to protect and guide their child. This is true regardless of who's paying for the cell phone plan, although more often than not it's the parents.

Parents might want to set times for when the phone can and cannot be used, having the child turn it off during the dinner hour, for example, or after a certain time, especially on school nights. They may lay down the rule that there is to be no cell phone use unless homework is finished. Parents should reserve the right to see call logs and texts, and to restrict access to the Internet if they wish. Other rules may be appropriate, especially for younger teens.

Parents should insist on certain expectations that go with having a cell phone (or any kind of personal technology). Teens are expected to maintain good grades and good conduct, for example, and to participate in family prayer time, to refrain from behavior such as bullying, bad language, or smoking, and so on.

For many parents (and young people), the cell phone can be a great means of communication. It is in my family. For reasons of safety and security, many parents will legitimately allow their children to have them. In most cases, however, I think that any child under the age of twelve is too young for a cell phone or other gadgets, such as an iPod. Until children show signs that they're capable of using a cell phone in a mature and ethical fashion, it's probably not a good idea to let them have one.

I should add that parents need to set a good example in how they themselves use their cell phones and other technology. If children see their parents being rude or constantly occupied with their cell phones, then the children will often exhibit this same behavior.

§§§

10.

What ethical considerations will help me guide
my son or daughter in regard to dating?

Or is it better to ask: Should they be allowed to date? I'm tempted to respond with the words of former First Lady Nancy Reagan's 1980s anti-drug message: "Just say no." Short of that advice, there's always the convent! All right, I'm just kidding.

In all seriousness, this question is of great ethical significance because of its bearing on the Sixth Commandment. Relationships with members of the opposite sex involve moral norms that rule out sexual activity before and outside of marriage. These relationships also call for such moral virtues as chastity and modesty, both of which fall under the virtue of temperance/moderation.

Still, if you were raised with the idea that dating at an early age was normal, then this question might seem peculiar. It's a good idea, however, to give this some thought and have a plan in mind so that you can guide your children when they raise the dating question. It's best to communicate early to the child, as he or she leaves the pre-teen years, that you will take a gradualist approach to this question. That is, as your child matures, he or she will of course gradually have more dealings with the opposite sex — planned and unplanned. The focus will be not so much on dating as on discerning one's *personal vocation* — one's distinctive way of being Jesus' disciple in the world. This will include discerning a call either to marriage, priesthood, religious life, or to single life in the world. But it will also include making sure that each and every one of our choices is conformed to and compatible with our personal vocations. And that includes choices that concern when and how we date.

The following stages are proposed simply as a general guide or road map, not as hard-and-fast rules. When the child is a high school freshman, at around the ages of thirteen or fourteen, the teenager may go to sporting events at school where he or she meets publicly in groups with other boys and girls. As a sophomore, around fifteen or sixteen years of age, the child can attend a school-sponsored dance where there are chaperones present. As a junior, around the ages of sixteen or seventeen, this same teen begins to find himself or herself drawn to more specific and exclusive relationships with someone of the opposite sex. (At this stage especially, parents need to continue to provide guidance and reminders about chastity, modesty, and respect for others.) As a high school senior, around seventeen to eighteen years of age, the young man or woman attends prom with a date who has the basic traits a Catholic would be looking for in a spouse. This doesn't mean that this date is the teen's future husband or wife, but that in the gradual process of discerning a vocation the teen has begun to prioritize those traits necessary to have a strong Christian marriage. By this age, the young person may not have a clear idea of the vocation God is calling him or her to but can be thinking seriously about the essentials needed for the particular vocation of marriage.

Parents are responsible for guiding their children through these stages, helping them discern wisely, and even, when the time comes, helping them discern a future mate.

It's possible, too, for a young man or woman to get to know a member of the opposite sex without having to date, or worse, hook up. A dating relationship can become too physically and emotionally intense and exclusive, bringing with it the potential for sex or a rush to marry, all of which can short-circuit the development of a mature, self-giving love. Parents must do their part to prevent their son or daughter from forming relationships that are too intimate, possibly by not allowing one-on-one dating until the teen is sixteen or seventeen and encouraging their teen to go out in groups. Parents know their children best and what approach works best with each child.

But the young person must keep in mind that in dating it is the good of *marriage* that he or she is discerning as a vocation. Anything beyond chaste expressions of affection is not at all morally appropriate, and it interferes with the discernment process itself, as well as the teen's academic studies and faith life. Thus, it is a good idea for parents to lay down certain specific rules — which may be modified at times — enabling the teenager to maintain sexual integrity. Basic rules would include, for example, that no member of the opposite sex can be over at your house without a parent or guardian present, no locked or closed doors when together, no sleepovers or overnight trips together, and so on. Of course, parents may need to set other rules or modify other rules in the best interest of their child, and they should always, when presenting and maintaining their rules, do so in a positive and loving way.

§§§

11.

How should a family best deal with an elderly parent whose driving skills are deteriorating?

Some readers might respond by saying, "Take away the keys!" Well, that would be one way of handling the situation, but of course a not too tactful or temperate one. Older people who rightly value their independence would most likely take great offense at the suggestion that they should no longer drive a car.

Whatever the reason, besides old age, for the diminished driving skills — Alzheimer's, blindness, side effects from medicines, and a host of other issues — losing the ability to drive and thus losing a great deal of independence and mobility is often a very difficult phase in the elderly person's life. It's one more concrete reminder that he is fragile and fated to die — and it can lead to depression and anger. In a very real sense, then, this is a moral and existential question, one that is probably more emotionally than intellectually difficult. It is a problem that all too many families have had to face or will face in the future.

If and when the elderly person's reduced motor skills and failing eyesight become evident (or preferably before then), it is time to discuss what to do about the situation. The driver can become a threat not only to his own life and property but also to the lives and property of others. I have driven with older drivers whose driving skills were getting weaker, and it was no joyride.

There are already enough distractions on the road — for example, drivers who are texting or talking on cell phones — without having to worry about elderly motorists who have become poor drivers. Indeed, in December 2011, I was involved in a hit-and-run accident when an elderly woman driving on a suspended license ignored a stop sign and, blind to my presence on the road, rammed into my new car's rear bumper. Afterward, the police said that there are too many such drivers on our roads and that they should be prohibited from driving. At the least, they need to have their driving skills reevaluated.

In order to make turning in the car keys and driver's license a bit easier, make sure that you've researched the alternatives available to your elderly parents or relatives so that you can show them that they will be able to get around by bus, taxi, subway, or by family, friends, and relatives offering rides. You must communicate to them, especially if they put up a fight, that you are doing this because you care for them and do not want to see them injured or killed, or see them injure and kill someone else.

Appeal to their moral conscience — that is, to their sense of what is right and wrong and best for everyone concerned. Speak to them in a way that will persuade them to freely consent to give up their car keys. Describe for them all that they stand to lose if they were the cause of a serious accident. The best-case scenario is for them to voluntarily agree to hand over their keys. Some experts recommend that you try to involve other professionals — for example, your parent's primary-care doctor, an ophthalmologist, the Department of Motor Vehicles, the family lawyer, and even the police, if necessary. All of these could help remove the elderly parent from the road by providing a variety of documentation as to driving skills, state of health, eyesight, coordination, and so on.

Your aging mother or father will be challenged to grow in the virtues of fortitude and patience. You as a son or daughter will need to grow in prudence as well as fortitude. As your parents lose their previous mobility, you and other siblings or neighbors may have to step up to the plate and assist them with running errands and taking them to church. But it can also be an occasion for spending more time with your parents, enabling you to grow in charity by helping them retain contact with the world outside their home. All this will help you grow in that practical wisdom so lauded in the Bible, the virtue that we've identified as prudence.

We need to protect society by keeping its roads safe for drivers and pedestrians. Thus, it definitely is morally imperative in many cases, in order to protect innocent people from being seriously harmed or killed, to notify the authorities that your aged father or mother has lost the skills necessary for operating a car safely and to take the keys from them when they refuse to give them up freely.

But we also must remember that at stake here is another supreme value that must be respected: the *dignity* of your mother and father in their old age. And as you will recall, there is a biblical commandment that says something about honoring that! (For more on the Fourth Commandment, see the *Catechism*, nn. 2197-2257.)

§§§

12.

Is body piercing or getting a tattoo a morally neutral act?

To all my friends and family out there who have tattoos or body piercings, the answer is no — it's not a morally neutral act. That doesn't mean that having or getting a tattoo or body piercing is morally bad. Actually, the Church has no official teaching on this question and hasn't said much about it one way or the other (Scripture is not conclusive either — see Leviticus 19:28). But obviously, any kind of alteration of the body involves a moral dimension.

To permanently or semi-permanently mutilate the body without a good reason is wrong. Sure, kidney transplants from live donors involve mutilation, but most would say that the reason is a good one, to save a life. As long as free and informed consent is given, it doesn't harm the donor in any serious way.

If it's your son or daughter who would like a tattoo, you have to ask why they want one. Simply to get a tattoo for reasons of vanity or to fit in with a certain crowd are probably not good reasons for anyone. (It is common for those in the military to have tatoos.) Having your ears pierced, however, is socially acceptable in our American culture, even for men (my twenty-two-year-old son has had his pierced). Tattoos that do not disfigure the human body, especially the face, seem okay as well. (My eighteen-year-old son has two tatoos on his arms.) More invasive and face-altering body piercings do not.

Nonetheless, even though cultural factors play a large role here, serious questions of a moral nature must be asked by anyone thinking of getting a tattoo or body piercing. Here are six of them for consideration.

First, could the money I am going to spend on a tattoo or minor body piercing be better spent on something else more essential for me or others?

Second, are there any risks to my health posed by these procedures? Ask yourself if the basic goods of health and bodily integrity are at stake with these actions to modify or enhance the human body (as they can be, for example, with breast augmentation surgery and bariatric surgery).

Third, what are the possible effects on my future employment if potential employers frown on or ban tattoos because they believe it will hurt their business or for other reasons?

Fourth, what does my tattoo or body piercing say about my moral character as a person? In the recent past, most people who had tattoos in our society were members of gangs or in prison. Even though the stigma of having a tattoo has largely worn off, still, for many people, tattoos bring a host of negatives. These negatives could very well increase — and the tattoo would be morally wrong — if it is sexually explicit, glorifies violence, is satanic in nature, or has a message that is crass or crude. If this is the case, then rather than communicate God's love, the tattoo could lead others into sin and thus seriously compromise the holiness and evangelical witness to which all Christians are called.

Fifth, unless I am able to get my tattoo removed later on if I so desire (a painful and expensive procedure in most cases), what is it going to look like on my body when I'm old? The question of beauty and aesthetics is not only for later in life but also for right now — although most people probably don't want to think about a tattoo grown old!

Many see in the increased phenomenon of tattooing and body piercing a glorification of "thug life" as well as a de-beautifying of our culture, even though those who get tats see them quite differently, even as an art form. Of course, a person could also rightly get a tattoo to cover up a birthmark or other bodily "defect," somewhat similar to victims of breast cancer who have breast reconstruction surgery after a mastectomy. In the latter case, the doctor is correcting in human nature what disease had corrupted.

Finally, sixth, where is the tattoo or body piercing going to be? On your back, hidden from view, or on the upper breast for everyone to see and ogle and where it will serve as a temptation to the sin of lust? Or will it be on one's forehead to serve commercially as a human "walking billboard" (some companies have actually used tattoos in their marketing efforts). Talk about turning the human body into a commodity! But the body is not a commodity; it is "a temple of the holy Spirit within you" (1 Corinthians 6:19). So, we are exhorted to "glorify God in [our] body" (1 Corinthians 6:20).

In any case, if we are talking about a minor child, the parents have the final authority on the matter. For children to purposely disobey their parents on this matter would be sinful, a violation of the Fourth Commandment.

§§§

13.

Are there any moral issues concerning pet ownership or even whether you can own a pet?

Well, yes, more than you might think at first glance. There are many good reasons for someone to own a pet — and I'm not referring to a monkey or a mountain lion. Having a dog or a cat in the home, for example, can:

- Provide companionship to young and old alike.
- Teach young children about responsibility.
- Offer protection to people and property.
- Aid the blind and other handicapped individuals.
- Provide assistance with household tasks.
- Provide entertainment for the owner when the pet participates in games and contests.

I personally can identify with the first two reasons, since my brother and I had both cats and dogs when we were growing up. Alas, my sister's allergies and my own forced our family to give away our animals, to our great sadness — accompanied by many tears.

I think today, however, many Americans look at pet ownership simply in terms of their own desires and wants. They do not always look at or are even aware of the many moral issues involved but simply accept the secular culture's attitude about pets. When I speak of moral issues, though, I am not primarily thinking of "animal rights" as spoken of by radically misguided groups such as People for the Ethical Treatment of Animals (PETA) and famous philosophers such as Peter Singer. Although there are ethical duties that we have toward animals because of the kind of beings *we* are (intelligent and free individuals), animals themselves do not have any rights. Of course, this denial of rights does not mean that we ought not to be kind to animals and avoid every cruelty and mistreatment of them, such as the practice of dog fighting. By no means! Nevertheless, we can use them, for example, in experiments that are geared toward finding cures for human diseases, especially when no other alternatives are available.

What about the Catholic Church? Does she offer any guidance on this question? She does, and some of it is quite specific. The *Catechism of the Catholic Church* affirms, "*Animals* are God's creatures" (n. 2416; emphasis in original). But it also notes that God has entrusted their care to the only creatures made in his image: men and women (see n. 2417). This is why it's legitimate to use animals for food and clothing, why they may be kept as pets to assist us in both work and play, and why they may be used in medical and scientific experimentation as long as this experimentation stays "within reasonable limits and contributes to caring for or saving human lives" (n. 2417).

The Catholic moral theologian Germain Grisez offers a fine summary of how we should think about the welfare of animals and how we should act toward them:

> The fact that animals, like all God's creatures, are good in themselves does not mean that their being and welfare are basic human goods, that is, reasons per se for human action. The moral goodness or sinfulness of human acts bearing on subhuman goods [e.g., animals] is determined by relevant human goods: religion (failure to respect the goodness of subhuman creatures is irreverent toward God) and fairness toward others (spoiling and wasting subhuman creatures almost always is likely to deprive others unreasonably of potential benefits). (*The Way of the Lord Jesus*, http://www.twotlj.org/G-3-92.html)

The *Catechism* further teaches:

It is contrary to human dignity to cause animals to suffer or die needlessly. It is likewise unworthy to spend money on them that should as a priority go to the relief of human misery. One can love animals; one should not direct to them the affection due only to persons. (n. 2418)

One of the best descriptions of how we are to regard animals, vis-à-vis humans, comes from the lips of Jesus himself, and so it reflects how God sees things: "Look at the birds in the sky; they do not sow or reap, they gather nothing into barns, yet your heavenly Father feeds them. Are not you more important than they?" (Matthew 6:26).

In this question, I am chiefly concerned with issues that pertain to pet ownership and justice toward human persons, and not those that relate to our treatment of nonrational animals themselves. And so for the remainder of my answer, I will focus on the last two sentences of what the *Catechism* teaches in paragraph 2418, above.

The *Catechism*, as we've seen, instructs us not to spend money on pets that should go to the alleviation of human suffering. Yes, we should show sympathy for animals and their welfare — even rescuing them and providing support for animal shelters. But the animals under our care are not people; they are pets. Domestic animals remain sub-personal realities, however much we have love and compassion for them. We may in fact, however, have an excessive emotional attachment to them that can cause problems if and when we need to part with them. (Of course, we can't predict whether we will develop such an out-of-proportion affection for the animal.) Because all this is so, individuals and families need to ask themselves in all honesty if they have an acceptable reason — not just an emotion or a feeling — for acquiring or keeping a pet.

Moreover, let's keep in mind that pets can use up scarce resources that could sometimes be put to better use toward the care of human beings, whether those resources are money, medical care, food, water, clothes, or whatever. In addition, pets can also have a negative impact on the environment in diverse ways, from the processes that go into feeding them to the destructive effects they have through the exercise of their bodily functions. (This would also include the noise, allergies, and injuries they may cause.) These are two additional but related problems of pet ownership that would require an acceptable countervailing reason to deflect these three negatives from ruling out pet ownership.

I don't want this conclusion of mine to sound overly strict or harsh. I'm not against pet ownership! I simply want to make the case for the moral dimension of pet ownership in general and the case against pet ownership specifically when there is no *adequate reason* — and genuine love of animals is such a reason — to justify it. My view is, in many ways, merely an extension or a fleshing-out of what the *Catechism* teaches.

§§§

14.
Is it morally okay for me to have a Facebook account?

Here's another sensitive question that we need to consider, especially today when social-networking sites are the way many people communicate. As with any technology, especially a new one, the question of its morally right use is one that needs to be raised. You may already be on Facebook or another social media site such as Twitter. If you are, then you're probably aware of some of the dangers.

First, I must confess that I have been on Facebook for several years and have found it to be both a wonderland and a wasteland. If you're already on Facebook, then I advise you to follow all of the moral principles and norms (for example, the Ten Commandments) that apply when you're off Facebook. For example, watch how much time you spend on it, possibly giving yourself a time limit; do not post any morally objectionable material, whether words, photos, or videos that, for example, could harm someone's good reputation (thus violating the Eighth Commandment) or constitute a sin against the Sixth Commandment; and try to use the medium to encourage what is morally good, even using it as a forum for evangelization. Doing this requires practicing virtues such as prudence and temperance, especially in terms of preserving and guarding a certain amount of your privacy online, as well as making sure not to waste too much time on the sites.

If you're not yet on Facebook, then ask yourself what *purpose* will it serve if you join? Here are some further questions that you may want to ask yourself before signing up, to help you discern what you should do: Do you want to stay in touch with family and friends by means of this site? Are you seeking wholesome friendship and fellowship? Do you want to keep up with what's going on in the world through this technology? Answering yes to any one or more of these is a good reason to have a Facebook account, if you so desire. Of course, as with any technology, there is always the possibility of getting addicted to it if you're not careful. You can't let your guard down.

Moreover, priests, deacons, and people in pastoral positions should be especially careful about who they "friend" and who they, in turn, accept as friends. Married men and women must be cautious as well, careful to avoid online affairs with girlfriends or boyfriends from the past. Sharing a password with your spouse might be an option for married couples, allowing access to each other's account and contacts. In general, a good piece of advice is: Don't tempt your virtue. If you think you're crossing a line, don't cross it. And try to go on social-networking sites at times when others in your family can see what you're viewing and posting. This will serve as a check and keep you honest with yourself. (I realize that many can connect with social-media sites on their smartphones, which makes this access easier.)

Finally, pre-teens should not, in my view, have their own personal Facebook accounts. They can get into too much trouble if allowed to be on Facebook unsupervised, especially since they are prone to temptations that they will not know how to handle at their young age. The phenomenon of online bullying is just one example of those troubles, but there are other problems beyond safety concerns as well, which I'm sure you've heard reported in the media.

Technology, such as Facebook, is merely a tool. It does not come with a moral manual explaining its proper moral uses. For that, we must turn to ethics, and specifically the moral virtues.

§§§

15.
Can I have a clear conscience while working for an employer or company engaged in morally wrong activities?

The answer to this question depends on what kind of wrong is being done and whether your employer is engaged in the moral wrong in his official capacity as head of the company or organization, or in his personal life. Clearly, if the company as a whole is engaged in work that is in itself evil, you cannot in good conscience work there. For example, a nurse is morally prohibited from working at Planned Parenthood because a large portion of their business is devoted to contraception and abortion — both intrinsically evil actions.

If an individual employer is engaged in wrongful activities in her personal life — for example, your boss is cheating on her husband — this would not in most cases be relevant to your continued employment at the company, even though what she is doing is intrinsically evil as well. (It may, however, have a bearing on whether you would *want* to work for such a person!)

The more difficult case arises when you are working for an employer who is running a legitimate business but is also engaged in morally illegitimate activity as part of that company — practicing fraud or money laundering, for example. Workers are often punished in various ways for revealing these immoral activities, but a patchwork of state and federal "whistleblower" laws exists to protect individuals who speak up and bring to light immoral and illegal activity in the government, the military, and the corporate world. These laws are complex, however, and differ from state to state.

If your work is directly contributing to the wrongdoing, then of course you have an obligation to stop doing it. This would be the case especially when, for example, you're aware that the company is knowingly selling a defective product that could cause harm or you know that your boss is embezzling money. If you're not directly facilitating the evil but do have it within your power to expose it or otherwise stop it, then you are responsible for doing so. Of course, your job may be in jeopardy if you speak up. You should first consult an attorney and ascertain what types of laws exist in your state to protect your whistleblowing. You may also want to speak with trusted fellow employees. In addition, you may also need to produce some clear-cut and substantial evidence of wrongdoing.

Whether you can have a clear conscience or not in this situation depends on several factors that may or may not be in play. Much more could be said about this question in terms of the principle of cooperation — material and formal — with evil. But we will leave that alone.

§§§

16.

Can I, without doing wrong, recommend a colleague for promotion who uses company time for personal activities?

This question and the next one may have some similarities with question fifteen in that they involve wrongdoing on the job, although that wrongdoing here may be minor, unintentional, or even only occasional. In this case, your colleague is doing personal tasks on the company dime. If this person is in a public sector position and performing personal business when expected to be on the job, then he or she may be cheating the taxpayer as well as the employer. I say "may be cheating" because many public jobs involve activities that can blend both the personal and the professional. For example, a policeman who engages in conversation with young people on a street corner seems to be doing something that we wouldn't want to say is simply wasting the taxpayers' money. He's actually performing an essential task of good police work: getting to know the citizens of the community he's policing.

It's true that some companies (Google is particularly famous for this) permit a certain amount of time on the job beyond lunch or break time for strictly personal activities, such as engaging in a short phone conversation with your spouse or playing a game of cards or video games. They may even encourage it as one way to keep their employees happy, stress free, creative, and productive.

Some jobs in the private sector (as with those in the public) involve the kind of work that is hard to separate into categories of personal time and company time. There can be overlap. For instance, factory work, where you punch in every day from seven to three, is very different from academic work, where some days you won't be teaching a class but will be working in your office and doing any number of different tasks, both personal and professional. As someone who had a Monday through Friday full-time summer job working in a paint factory for seven consecutive summers and who now teaches in a seminary, I can testify to this difference in styles of work. In factory work, you seem to be always on the job, despite the fact that there can be downtime.

In many companies, however, the attitude seems to be, as long as you get your work done and you're productive, it doesn't matter whether you occasionally check Facebook while you're writing your next book (as I am doing right now). My brother Chris, who is a manager at a large international company, informs me of a helpful distinction to keep in mind: that of salary exempt vs. salary non-exempt (hourly employees). Salary exempt employees often stay late, take their job home with them, or work while traveling for the company. They are always on the clock but aren't eligible for overtime pay. It's pretty much accepted that these employees have more flexibility with their time, and personal tasks such as occasional web surfing are tolerated as long as personal time isn't abused. In the long run, the company comes out ahead with the amount of time the employee gives back at odd hours.

Of course, this kind of flexibility is light-years away from the situation discovered at the Securities and Exchange Commission where, for five years, according to a 2010 federal report, over thirty well-paid, taxpayer-funded workers watched hours upon hours of pornography, not the stock market, on their government-supplied computers while the economy was melting down. Some jobs and professions permit little or no use of work time for personal time — airline pilots, bus drivers, and security guards, for example, when they are actively on the job. For a bank guard to be watching TV rather than the security screens by the vault violates the very nature of his job description: keeping people and property safe and secure. This is not a case of a guard performing his duties poorly; it's a case of him not performing them at all, thus putting people in harm's way and property at risk.

All this seems a long way from our original question, but it's necessary to do it justice. Obviously, if your colleague was doing something akin to what some of the SEC workers were doing, you would not recommend him for a promotion or a raise. In fact to do so, knowing what he had done, would be to engage in wrong-doing on your part. Indeed, in the example of the SEC workers, you would have a moral obligation to reveal any bad or illegal activity. This would be another case of the whistleblowing that we spoke of in question fifteen.

The bottom line would seem to be that if the employee was an otherwise good worker, had received good evaluations, was rarely late or absent, was cordial, and so on, then you could recommend your colleague for promotion as long as this worker's personal activities on the job met the following two criteria: (1) these personal activities did not in any significant manner interfere with his work in any way (its quality, the meeting of deadlines, safety, and so forth); (2) these personal activities did not lead fellow workers to think that substantial company time could be routinely used for non-work related business (unless of course that was allowed by company policy).

These two criteria are not so much clear-cut rules as guidelines. They help determine not only whether others are abusing company or government work time but also enable you to evaluate your own use of time while on the job. If you desire a simpler guide, the Golden Rule once again provides it: if you were the employer, would you mind if your employee took care of personal business on the job?

As we'll see in dealing with question twenty, "occasional use" is another principle that can be of assistance in helping us answer this question and related ones, since it addresses not only the use of company assets but also can be extended to deal with questions relating to the amount of time that you licitly (or illicitly) devote to personal business when on the job.

§§§

17.
How should I approach a situation where my boss or a co-worker occasionally takes credit for my ideas?

Talk about a delicate situation! This question has a bit of a resemblance to question fifteen but only if taking credit in this case involves *wrongdoing*. That's what we need to clarify.

As a general rule, people should not take credit for the work of others. That's pretty obvious to most people. When co-workers take credit for another person's ideas, it's not only unacceptable, it warrants a discussion with a manager or supervisor. If it continues, the human resources department can be brought into the discussion.

But things can get a bit complicated when we're talking about such professions as political speech writing or the work of Supreme Court justices or academic book writing, to cite just a few examples. These professions all involve some level of "taking credit" for the ideas or work of others: the politician "taking credit" for the work of the speech writer, the justice for the law clerk, the academic writer for the research assistant. In many, if not most cases, authors will rightly acknowledge the research assistance and writing of others. In other cases, it is understood by the public that the president's speech, for example, was not crafted solely by him; that he had a team of speechwriters work on it, but that ultimately, the president signed off on it, making it his own. A similar process is at work when a pope composes an encyclical or other magisterial document.

In professions such as advertising and finance where large sums of money are involved, or in science where there might be a question of patents, another layer is added to the question. Workers in a research facility who work as a team often share the fruits of their research, but the inventors or discoverers are not contractually able to claim ownership of the new product or process, or to benefit financially from it, at least not directly. It now belongs to the company that hired them.

My father, who was a paint chemist, had a patent for a product that was designed to refurbish the appearance of vinyl and other painted surfaces. Since my father was hired to come up with new products for the Flood Company in Hudson, Ohio, they were the true owners of his product and could rightly take credit for it.

Any products that my father came up with on his own time, with his own resources, as he did many times out in our garage on Normandy Avenue in Cleveland, Ohio, were his intellectual property and could have been marketed for financial gain without his having to share any of the profits with the company he worked for.

When, however, a co-worker or a boss takes credit for something, in effect passing it off as his own, possibly for reasons of promotion or profit, a bright line has been crossed. This, of course, can negatively affect your own prospects for advancement. But this is not only an injustice to you; it's also an injustice to the employer who ends up possibly rewarding the wrong person, the one who has stolen your idea(s).

What to do? If the guilty party is your boss and he has someone in authority over him, it may be possible to take the matter to this higher supervising authority. If it's a fellow co-worker, it may be possible to take the matter directly to your (mutual) boss. Obviously it's a good idea to make sure you can prove your charges. Hence, be sure to document your research or work, thus showing that you came up with these ideas, and not the person who claims to have done so.

People sometimes recommend that you plot a strategy to take advantage of the one who's taking advantage of you — that is, engage in some form of "payback." In this scenario, which would apply primarily to a boss, you try to engineer things in such a way that your boss "gets the picture" that you're tired of being taken advantage of—whatever this might look like. If it's possible to do so without risking one's job, a better strategy, however, might be to do as follows: You will continue to supply the boss with ideas, and he can continue taking some measure of credit for them, but you eventually tell him that you will expect some reward, some compensation from the company in return for your contribution, as only seems fair.

The former option is not a strategy that I would endorse without some serious reservations, unless it is carried out in a way that does not violate any moral norms, is not done in a threatening or hateful way, and is more or less a last resort, when all other avenues of redress have been exhausted. Why is that? Well, this approach can place you in a position of indignity, for you are, in a sense, playing hardball (some might say that's a nicer way of saying you're seeking revenge) and still letting your boss take credit for your ideas. Or if you threaten your boss with the exposure of his wrongdoing unless given something of value in return, then you're engaging in a form of blackmail, and that's morally wrong. But human beings, as individuals of immeasurable value, are not to be treated this way; that goes for your boss and for you. The one who takes advantage of his position of power in this way is also harmed in another sense: by so acting, the superior lessens his own dignity by giving himself the moral identity of an unjust and unfair person.

My brother Chris, a manager at a large company (as noted in question sixteen), says that the problem of managers or supervisors "stealing" ideas from subordinates can be a gray area. If a worker tells his boss: "Hey Bob, I've got this great idea to increase productivity for the company," and Bob passes it along to *his* boss but fails to credit the worker, my brother tells me that the worker wouldn't have much recourse. The employee works for him, he's the boss, and the idea is, in a way, the company's idea. The worker might not like his boss for doing this, but there's not much he can do about it.

In the long run, in a situation where others take credit for your ideas, it's best to offer the ideas in discussion with multiple people present so that you have witnesses.

Of course, most companies have a process where formal complaints can be filed confidentially with human resources, and the matter is then adjudicated internally. This becomes an especially exigent matter whenever the taking credit for ideas becomes more frequent, it is your boss who is doing it, and you're receiving absolutely no credit whatsoever. It may also involve the blatant theft of ideas. This could indicate a situation where the idea thief is stealing or taking credit for the ideas of others as well, not just yours. Sometimes, as a last resort, the only way to address the problem is by filing a lawsuit.

The principles (and virtues) of fairness, justice, and truth-telling are all in play in dealing with this question: showing fairness to the idea-generator; bringing justice to the offender (this may well involve some form of punishment); getting justice for the aggrieved; and truth-telling on the part of both.

§§§

18.
Is it ever morally okay to get paid "under the table"?

This is a real tough one! It involves morality, tax law, the underground economy, and a host of other issues. I will try to keep my answer simple — simple, but I hope not simplistic! Rather than deal with companies and corporations (or illegal immigrants, though this topic particularly affects them), I approach the question primarily from the standpoint of the individual worker who is a citizen of the United States.

The moral theologian Germain Grisez hints at an answer — one I agree with — when he observes:

> The New Testament instructs Christians to pay taxes [he cites the following Gospel texts: Matthew 22:15-22, Mark 12:13-17, and Luke 20:20-26], and this moral instruction is still handed on by the Church's teaching [he cites the *Catechism of the Catholic Church*, nn. 2238-2240, among other references]. Though part of the money raised by taxation is used in doing evil, citizens generally may and should pay legally required taxes to support the good things government does. (*The Way of the Lord Jesus*, http://www.twotlj.org/G-3-169.html) (This is another instance of material cooperation with evil that can be justified — indeed, that is morally required.)

People who are formally hiring household help — for example, a nanny or babysitter, even if just part-time — should consult the Department of the Treasury/Internal Revenue Service's *Household Employer's Tax Guide*, which provides the U.S. government's law on your tax responsibilities to those you hire. Individuals such as teenagers who are trying to determine whether they need to file a federal tax return on cash payments that they received from, say, occasional babysitting, mowing lawns, or painting houses for neighbors in the summer, should see the IRS's chart listing the filing requirements for most taxpayers.

Because getting paid under the table or off the books can be fraught with so much confusion, the Consumer Jungle website wisely advises:

- To protect yourself, report all income you earn on your tax return, no matter how it was received.
- A good rule of thumb is that if you are a steady, long-term employee earning more than $600, your employer should report your earnings and provide you with a government form that outlines your earnings.
- If you are ever put in a situation where an employer wants to pay you under the table, insist that you would be more comfortable if you were not paid in that manner. (http://consumerjungle.org/jungle-talk/under-the-table)

This third point is particularly important. You do not want to engage in anything illegal by failing to pay any taxes that ought to be paid, and you do not want to be put into a situation where you will not be eligible for certain benefits that are contingent on your employer paying taxes on you (for example, Social Security).

Now, at this point you may be saying to yourself, "Isn't this taking things a bit too far? I'm all for paying taxes, but this sounds a bit extreme." But remember that we're not talking about smaller amounts of money that your non-professional neighborhood family babysitter makes — even those that go a few dollars over the $600, but that under $600 no tax need legally be paid anyway. We're only talking about cash payments that go beyond the threshold of what the government deems taxable income in a given year — for example, businesses hiring full- or part-time workers and paying them under the table in cash.

Sure there is a compelling case to be made for the argument that says that if employers have to report their employees' earnings to the government, no one will want to go through the hassle of taking babysitting or lawn-cutting or handyman jobs anymore — and no one will want to formally hire such workers for regular work either. The underground economy is a large portion of Third World economies and makes up a significant percentage of our own. Much can be said in its favor in developing nations, especially when government red tape makes starting a business there extremely costly and difficult. But in our democratic capitalist country, where conditions are very different than in the Third World, many would take the argument in a different direction: that the informal underground economy is vital to households and neighborhoods trying to stay above the poverty line or barely clinging to the middle class.

Nonetheless, not paying your taxes is usually unfair to the majority of those who do, though one can grant that those who are truly in dire straits — the waitress with a large family struggling to make ends meet as a single mother — could make a case for not declaring money received under the table, such as tips, as income, at least that portion that helps her stay afloat. (I am aware that there is debate on the question of how much the poor actually pay in income taxes: from either nothing to a certain percentage when state and local taxes paid by the working poor are included.)

For those interested in further information, the Bloomberg Businessweek website presents a brief but interesting debate regarding the pros and cons of the underground economy — that is, under-the-table pay — in an article entitled "Under-the-Table Pay is Unacceptable."

For those required to pay taxes, I conclude that income tax evasion is, in addition to being illegal, both morally wrong and economically wrongheaded, even if there are strong incentives for both workers and businesses to engage in the practice, and even if there are many who do it for various reasons, some good, some bad. Only under certain very limited and restricted conditions could it be morally legitimate to withhold paying income taxes or a portion thereof (for example, as a protest against certain government actions such as abortion or war or other grave violations of human rights). As far as not paying income taxes on money received under the table, only in the kind of situations I have laid out do I think it could possibly be allowed, and not with large sums of money.

§§§

19.

Can I without guilt call in sick to work when I'm really just taking the day off?

To answer this question, we need to recall the great value of truth and truth-telling, and the immorality of lying (see question six), as well as the value of keeping commitments and contracts. For Christians, this value takes on added significance because Jesus called himself "the way and the truth and the life" (John 14:6). And so, as an employee, you should call in sick when and only when you are really sick. And when you are sick and would have had to work, you are grateful for sick days and the opportunity to stay home and rest!

Of course, most companies grant a certain number of sick days and personal days. Also, many companies are in fact flexible in what they regard as a sick day. For example, some will allow you in good faith to call in sick when you have a sick child or parent at home to care for. Many employees, however, might simply take a personal day or even a vacation day to deal with these situations, if those are available. These options are morally sounder than picking up the phone and calling in sick to work when one really *isn't* sick. This is especially true when your presence at work may be urgently needed on that day. The burden of the extra work may simply fall, unfairly, on someone else.

Then too, there must be a dialogue of some sort — both formal and informal — between the employer and the employee on this matter. That is, the employer should communicate flexibility with respect to sick time (if that is, in fact, the case). Employers must also express their expectation that the common good of the company — another value shared by all — will be honored by the employee. And the employee, in turn, should be given the freedom to express such ideals as the desire that their business or place of employment be family-friendly and respectful of the dignity and rights of the worker.

While people call in sick for all sorts of reasons, it's not something that you can do guilt-free, unless you are, well, *sick*. How sick is something that can be left up to individual workers and their conscience — they know best if it's a case of being too sick to work or simply sick of work! (Although, the company might want a doctor's excuse in cases where, among other reasons, there is cause to doubt the employee.) But sure, a sick day may extend to a so-called mental health day too, as managers have told me, for example, when you've been working day and night on a big project or you've been through a family crisis.

The lesson is that even in this area of our lives — our work — the moral law is *on*; it doesn't rest or call in sick.

§§§

20.

Is it morally all right for me to use a company printer (or other property) for personal matters on occasion?

This is a practice that goes on quite frequently, I am sure, usually undetected, as we'll see. It may be a printer or it may be some other piece of company property or equipment. If on one or two occasions you've run off a few copies on the office printer, especially when you're in a hurry, that's probably okay if your company follows the principle known in workplace ethics as occasional use. But if it's something that you do with moderate to excessive frequency, then it is a form of stealing, whether you want to call it that or not. It also becomes time spent away from doing the job your employer is paying you for — another form of theft.

I think it's a good idea to ask your supervisor if it's okay for you to use the printer for personal use on this particular occasion or occasions. But you have to keep in mind that you're probably not the only employee using the printer for personal use, with or without permission. One June 2008 survey reported that 60 percent of Canadians were doing so, with their personal printing including items such as maps, directions, e-mails, and photos.

The once or twice printing of copies that you do can easily begin to escalate to larger jobs of greater regularity, even if unintentional, at least at first. Hey, you might think, "It's better than using up the expensive inkjet in my printer at home!" Resist that thought, however tempting it might be.

It's a different case altogether if those personal pages that you're putting through the photocopier also somehow happen to be business copies — as, for instance, when you run off a map and driving directions to go to a business appointment that will be followed with dinner at a nearby restaurant with a friend. If this is true, then it seems to me that there is no conflict at all. Having such a dual purpose here does not make the act of copying on the company printer wrong but rather can actually make it right.

It might also be the case that you have been given the green light to use the company printer with the understanding that you will reimburse the company for the paper (and maybe the ink and toner) that you use. But then again, maybe you haven't been given the green light. In the end, you really need to check the company policy before proceeding, especially when it's an expensive print job.

It may also be the case that your printer at home may not be capable of doing certain jobs or you may not have one or have access to one. But these days, printers and ink are not all that expensive for most people. (Many spend as much on entertainment in a month.) If you find yourself tempted to make copies at work, then it's time to purchase and use a home printer or seek out a generous friend's printer.

The Global Ethics University website has an interesting article about this topic, "Company Assets and Occasional Use." The author, Mark S. Putnam, points out that *good judgment* is needed in order to exercise the principle of occasional use well, and he provides useful guidelines for how to apply it. To speak of sound judgment is really another way of speaking of the virtue of prudence that we have insisted on in all of our questions.

§§§

21.

Is it appropriate for me to retire at an early age and begin receiving a pension and then take another job?

Here's another very complicated question that we'll have to keep simple, leaving many important issues aside. First, let's look at the economic big-picture. There seem to be three models for dealing with the U.S. debt and financial crisis: (1) raising taxes, (2) making spending cuts, or (3) some combination of both. There is a fourth, do nothing, but it doesn't seem all that common as a realistic model.

One side argues that in today's weakened and debt-ridden economy, both here and globally, it is becoming extremely difficult to honor the promises made to workers years ago by politicians, union bosses, and management during much better economic times. Nevertheless, those same workers made future plans based on those promises that would guarantee them a certain amount of fixed income and a decent health care plan in their retirement years. As a matter of justice, it would seem that those contracts, however outlandish by today's economic outlook, would need somehow to be honored for those retired or soon to retire.

But one can also see the other side's argument: federal, state, and local governments are going broke, and there is not enough money to provide these future retirees their full pensions. When you throw in health care for these public-sector workers, these unfunded liabilities come to a staggering figure in the trillions of dollars. Some state governments have attempted to get public sector unions, for example, to pay a higher percentage of their pensions and health care, as happened in Wisconsin with Gov. Scott Walker's entitlement-reform proposals, to great backlash. (It's also not uncommon today to read about cities declaring bankruptcy — Detroit, where I work, being the most famous so far.)

And the same is true of various entitlement-reform proposals coming from various sectors of the federal government, whose purpose it is to deal with our nation's debt by reforming such programs as Social Security and Medicare, while also hopefully saving them (for example, the so-called "Ryan Plan" of Rep. Paul Ryan [R-WI] and the report of the National Commission on Fiscal Responsibility and Reform — that is, the so-called Bowles-Simpson Report). We can sum up this side's argument this way: We're broke and can no longer pay for lavish pensions or fund these entitlement programs — at least not the way we've been doing in the past. Therefore, in the words of the bipartisan Bowles-Simpson debt-commission report: "Don't make promises we can't keep." (For the full report, significantly titled *The Moment of Truth*, go to the government's fiscal-commission website.

Now, we won't be able to settle these political problems here, but the discussion puts our question in a larger context. As for the "small picture," that is, you the individual worker, I would encourage you and every person asking this question to consider not only your own economic well-being, but that of the community and country, trying to do *what you are able to do* to contribute to solving our nation's financial mess — however little that might be. This concern for the common good is an exercise of the virtues of solidarity and social justice. There is enough blame to go around, but the time for blaming has passed. The doomsday debt clock is ticking, the experts tell us.

All citizens in this situation, then, must ask themselves if they could pay more for their health care or their pensions (even if temporarily) in order to stabilize the debt and help bring fiscal health to their company, their city, their county, their state. People may well have to realize that promises made to them, while they *ought* to be honored, cannot *always* be honored, without fault being attributed to those who break them. "Conditions on the ground change," as the military saying goes. There is no moral absolute that promises be kept in each and every circumstance, especially of course when they are immoral. In a time of war or national disaster, some promises will indeed be broken. (I grant that one can very well ask if this money that was promised has been managed properly and wisely by those entrusted with it.)

Even though the retirement age is being raised, workers who can still retire early and then begin receiving a pension need to ask themselves if that is always a good thing: it may or it may not be. If you are going to retire in your forties or fifties only to take another job, while also receiving a pension from your first job (that is, double-dipping), then that model seems to be contributing to our financial woes and is not a sustainable one going forward. I realize that there are many exceptions: some employees are required for sound reasons to retire at a certain age (FBI special agents, for example, by federal law have a mandatory retirement age of fifty-seven); illness or injury can change financial situations overnight; some workers have large families to feed and educate; and so on.

We come back to the Golden Rule. It compels me to ask: "Is my early retirement fair?" Fair to this current generation of the middle-aged and of the young who will have to foot the bill for my and others' entitlements? Fair to those who seek jobs but are unable to find them because I (and others) have taken a job in "retirement"? Fair to the city or company that might go bankrupt or close because of unsustainable or unfunded liabilities?

I understand that there may be very good and legitimate reasons to retire early and begin collecting a pension. You may have planned on doing charitable work or missionary work. You may have been counting on that excellent health care plan to care for sick family members. Maybe you were going to adopt a child. Or maybe you had planned on going back to school to become a nurse or doctor. Divorce or the death of a spouse may have upset your present and future economic forecasts. We could go on with these scenarios.

Of course, much by way of policy and programs will be out of your hands. You can vote and make your voice heard in any number of ways, but what you end up having as pension benefits is left up to forces largely beyond your control. What will be, will be. But it's a good idea to begin today thinking about these questions, especially if you are not yet faced with retirement. I'd like you to begin seeing this question not simply in economic terms but in moral terms, both your side and the other side. What can I give up? What can I sacrifice? What am I being called to do? What will I do in my early retirement: simply amuse myself or use my time well? Will I not only rightly enjoy myself but also contribute in some significant way to the good of my family, my friends, my community, and my Church?

Public-sector workers need to remember that it is the taxpayer who is funding their salaries and pensions. And so, when people say that government needs to tighten its belt and cut spending, it implies that government workers as well as programs will take a financial hit. Whether we are speaking of a union or a company, both need to ask what is good for the *common good*.

Do the authentic rights of workers have to be respected? Yes, absolutely. Magisterial teaching and the Catholic social justice tradition say as much. But in today's radically changed economic environment, asking some public-sector workers to pay what their private-sector counterparts are and have been paying for years seems neither unreasonable nor does it seem to constitute an infringement on their rights in every case — and we have to have clarity on precisely what those are. But governments and employers will also have to do their part to: reform the tax code; eliminate waste and fraud; reward both innovation and ethical behavior; and engage in the belt tightening they are asking of workers. (Maybe members of Congress and CEOs can cut their own pay and campaign less!)

For many, whether convinced by my analysis or not, this will be a bitter pill to swallow. I understand and can sympathize with these people. Many are my family members and friends.

Besides the principle of the Golden Rule and the virtue of solidarity, all of the cardinal moral virtues will be called for: prudence, for you to discern the right financial decisions to make; justice, to make sure that all concerned parties have their rights respected and are given their due; fortitude, to have the courage to stand up to violations of your rights; and patience, to withstand economic difficulties and bear any economic sufferings well; and finally, temperance — that is, self-control or moderation in your spending or consumer habits.

§§§

22.

Is it morally wrong not to tip a waiter or waitress in a restaurant?

This is another question that involves in a particular way the virtue of justice — that virtue that is most "other" directed. The answer depends on a number of factors, including what country you are in (in some countries — for example, Germany — you don't tip). There are many workers who rely on tips — such as barbers, hairdressers, bellboys, parking valets, shoeshine workers, carwash attendants, bartenders, delivery boys, massage therapists, party-bus drivers, and taxicab drivers, to name some of the most common, although some of these rely on tips more so than others. I will focus on the waiter and waitress group of workers and will presume that, by virtue of the fact that you are eating out at a restaurant, whether expensive or inexpensive, you can afford to tip. I realize that is not always true, but I will assume it is so here.

It seems to me that there is no absolute positive duty that says we have to tip in every situation. For example, some waiters and waitresses are not very good at the job, or they are not at the top of their game when waiting on you on a particular night for whatever reason — and so you don't leave a tip as a way of indicating that the service was poor. Even in this situation, however, it's better to show kindness (and mercy!) and leave a small tip (say, 10 percent), simply informing the waiter in a friendly but firm manner of your dissatisfaction. If it happens on a second and third visit, it might be time to say something to the management, for your sake and the other customers. It may turn out, however, that the poor service was not the fault of your waiter but was due to other causes.

Sometimes, to mention another scenario, you mistakenly do not bring enough money to cover both the tip and the meal. In this situation, it's a good idea, in order to avoid any injustice and your own embarrassment, to leave a large tip the next time you're in. I'm sure that there are other circumstances that would justify not tipping the waitress or waiter, but these, I think, would be few and far between.

Nevertheless, we know that these workers depend on the tips that they receive to pay bills, tuition, rent, and so on. Many of them are making much less than the minimum wage or a just wage. Moreover, waiters and waitresses often have to "tip out" a percentage of their tips to the busboys for every table that they've served — and so, when you don't tip, you also shortchange them. These folks are often working in these jobs precisely because of the good money that they can make on tips. My college-age son, for example, who works part-time as a dryer in a carwash, is paid nowhere near a minimum wage. When he is not tipped well, his earnings for that day are pitiful. But even when the carwash has a good day in tips, he still has to evenly split all of the tips he has collected with the other dryers — and sometimes there are three or four of them.

A strong case can be made for saying that tipping is not only a matter of custom in our country but also of one's moral responsibility to help the working poor and others earn a just wage. Customers should not only tip but also give a generous gratuity. This is usually considered to be, at a minimum, 15 percent of your bill, up to 20 percent. But there is no set limit on how much you can tip. We should tip munificently when able, not only out of gratefulness and appreciation for a job well done, but we should also tip well as a matter of justice.

You will also most likely find that simply as a matter of self-interest you will receive better service on subsequent visits when you tip generously, over those patrons who do not tip so lavishly. Of course, this raises questions of fairness and justice. This is one reason why some authors suggest getting rid of the practice of tipping altogether and replacing it with a just wage.

To my mind, some bad reasons for tipping would be those revealed in a CNNMoney website article "Tipping Not Optional": to feel less guilty about being waited on, to reduce the envy the waiter might feel for your better financial situation, and to avoid the social stigma of being considered a cheapskate.

§§§

23.
Do I have a moral responsibility to say something to a friend who is living with a girlfriend or boyfriend, and if so, what should I say?

"Don't do it!" Okay, you need to say more than that. Like questions twenty-four and twenty-five, this is a sensitive moral issue that must be handled firmly but delicately. Once again, because we have a case of sex outside of the marriage covenant, there's a clear violation of the Sixth Commandment, as it has been understood by the Catholic Church. God gives us this commandment to protect both the dignity of the couple as well as the dignity of any possible child that may come to be, as a fruit of their, in this case, non-marital union.

In my answer, I'll presume that you're a close friend of the cohabitator(s). I believe that the best approach to this question is one which shows concern rather than condemnation, even though what they are doing is objectively wrong — whether they know it or not.

Tell your friend that you care about his physical, emotional, social, spiritual, and moral well-being. If your friend is a Christian, you can also address the Bible's teaching on fornication — that is, sex outside of marriage, and its detrimental effect on the spiritual life. St. Paul is very clear that fornicators will not inherit the Kingdom of God (see 1 Corinthians 6:9). Because the body is the "temple of the holy Spirit" (1 Corinthians 6:19), sexual sins strike particularly deeply against the body (see 1 Corinthians 6:18).

There is the slight possibility that a person is living with a girlfriend or boyfriend but not having sex in the relationship. The couple may even be engaged to be married and are living together to save money or to overcome the problem a long-distance relationship poses. Surely, that's a better situation than a one-night stand, but nevertheless still morally wrong.

Whatever the reason, and whether sexual relations are taking place or not, the couple should also consider the matter of scandal, which doesn't refer to shock or outrage but rather to leading others into sin through one's bad behavior which serves as a "green light" to others. And that's exactly what it is: bad behavior, regardless of the fact that everyone seems to be doing it these days.

If the couple is in fact planning to marry, you should also cite the extensive research showing that those who live together before marriage are greatly disadvantaged in their ability to have both a happy marriage and a permanent one. Most people are unaware of these studies on the negative impact of cohabitation on marriage, child-rearing, and family well-being, but you can find information in this regard on the United States Conference of Catholic Bishops website and elsewhere. In sum, "playing house" is not the best way to "play" at marriage.

Most dioceses require at least a six-month period of marriage preparation for all couples who want to marry in the Church, encouraging the cohabitating couple to live separately until they are married.

Your friend needs to ask himself whether he is ready to receive a child into the relationship, should a pregnancy occur outside of marriage. Would the temptation be there to abort the child or harm the child in some way after birth? The instability of a sexual relationship outside the bond of marriage makes for a rocky home life both before and after marriage, for the child and the couple. Given the clear and overwhelming evidence of the danger that "living in sin" (to use an older expression) poses to the stability and happiness of one's possible future marriage, to risk such a pre-marital sexual relationship constitutes an immoral experiment: maybe we'll be one of the few lucky ones whose marriage works out okay, but maybe we won't be so lucky and it won't work out okay.

Last but not least, whether your friend has much Christian faith, little faith, or no faith at all, you can suggest he read about

Pope John Paul II's marvelous teaching on the theology of the body.

One aspect of this teaching notes that the human body not only *has* but indeed *is* a "language" that expresses the person as either male or female. An aspect of that language includes the act of sexual intercourse. As the most intimate of all bodily acts, capable of expressing the goods of both love and life, it "says" something to the other: "I love you forever with all my heart, soul, and body, and I want to start a family with you." That "other" can only be one's spouse, the one that you have irrevocably committed yourself to in the bond of marriage.

Fornicators, however, "say" something other than the language of committed love that's open to life. They often try to say one thing with their *bodies* ("I want to share love and my entire life with you"), while not having made the definitive and irrevocable *choice* ("I do") to allow that act to express its full truth and authentic meaning as committed conjugal love. In a sense, then, their bodies do not speak the truth of their situation, but a lie.

If your friend is a Catholic, you can also steer him to some of the Church's documents that address this issue head-on, such as *Persona Humana* (1975), *Familiaris Consortio* (1981), and the *Catechism of the Catholic Church* (1997). These are all available on the Vatican website.

§§§

24.

Is it morally justifiable to attend a wedding ceremony of a man and a woman who have cohabitated?

Didn't we just have a question on cohabitation? We sure did. But in this case, it's a matter of whether you should be present at the wedding ceremony of a couple that has been cohabitating. So the reality is the couple has been living together but is now going to get married — it's a done deal. We will presume that the couple in question is marrying according to the laws of the Church.

One concern is obviously the question of scandal — the leading of others into sin by conveying the message that either your sinful behavior or that of another is not in fact morally wrong. Would your presence at the wedding somehow constitute a bad example by implying that you approve of cohabitation or have no moral objection to it?

There's nothing in the Church's canon law that legislates on this particular issue. That being said, our concern is primarily moral rather than canonical. But what's the best course of action, especially if you are close friends or family or relatives of the co-habitating couple?

As we saw in question twenty-three, your response to this question depends much on your relationship to the couple and several other factors. We have noted that what used to be called living in sin or fornication is no longer looked upon as something morally wrong by many today. It's considered normal, routine, the best way to get to know if this person is right for you — that is, if you are compatible. But neither the Church nor most social science agrees with this viewpoint, as we also noted.

Different people will arrive at different judgments of conscience in regard to this question. I think one could argue that if the wedding is going to be a big affair, especially where you will know many people, then a conscientious decision not to attend the wedding but attend the reception could be justified based on the fear of scandal (though some might well wonder if it's even possible to scandalize people who have rejected much of the moral teachings of the Church on sex). Some might flip the two events and argue that they will attend the wedding, but skip the reception. Others will take the position that they will attend both events regardless of how big the wedding is and regardless of how many people they know will be there. They argue that their presence does not mean they countenance any kind of immoral behavior.

Those who argue in favor of attending, especially if it's a close family member or friend, usually will say that they have made their views on pre-marital sex very clear to the engaged couple in private conversation. They note that they have decided that it would be better to attend, not as a statement of approval of their cohabitation but of an affirmation of their marriage and future life together as a married couple. In this way, they avoid alienating the couple, and they keep the lines of communication open. Thus, they are better situated to keep evangelizing the couple after the nuptials. People who argue along these lines will often say further that this is especially the case if the couple has decided to keep their wedding a private ceremony, with just family and a few invited guests, with the same being true of the reception.

Again, good reasons can be put forward for either attending or staying home. But these reasons should be based on the most effective way to witness — both to the couple and to any who may be influenced by your decision — to the Church's and the Gospel's teaching on the full truth about marriage and sex. You will need the virtue of prudence — and this *is* very much a prudential matter — to determine not only the right response but also the best one in the given circumstances. So, too, you will need prayer to the Holy Spirit for the gift of wisdom. Whatever course of action you decide to take, it should be done in a spirit of charity for all those concerned.

§§§

25.

What do I say to divorced and civilly remarried Catholics whose first marriage has not been annulled, but who are nonetheless still receiving Holy Communion?

My first thought is a question: Do you know this couple well enough to speak with them about such a delicate matter? If you don't, then it may be more appropriate for the pastor to deal with the situation. But if you do know the couple well, then you may want to arrange to meet privately, in a comfortable setting, to tell them how much you truly care about them and their situation, and want to help resolve it. Of course, this *is* a sensitive and difficult issue — otherwise it wouldn't have made my list of questions! But at its heart, it's also a *moral* question because of the right moral conduct and disposition necessary for worthily receiving the sacrament of the Eucharist. The Catholic Church, following Sacred Scripture, teaches that one may not receive the Body of Christ if one is aware of having committed a mortal sin (see 1 Corinthians 11:27), such as adultery. It becomes an ethical issue for *you* if you know the couple's situation and are aware that they are receiving Communion.

You could tell your friends that they should seek out the annulment process in their diocese to deal with their prior bond — that is, to inquire whether their first marriage may be annulled. If they're at least striving to be faithful Catholics, you may also gently quote to them the words of Jesus condemning divorce and remarriage as adultery (see Matthew 5:31-32 and parallels). You should also refer them to the clear, authoritative teaching of the Catholic Church, as found in such documents as Pope John Paul II's apostolic exhortation on the Christian family in the modern world — *Familiaris Consortio* (n. 84) — and more recently in the letter from then-Cardinal Ratzinger concerning the reception of Communion by divorced and remarried Catholics (*Letter to the Bishops of the Catholic Church Concerning the Reception of Holy*

Communion by the Divorced and Remarried Members of the Faith-
ful, 1994). Both can be found on the Vatican website. Don't presume your friends are familiar with these documents.

But you must also communicate to them the fact that the
Church greatly sympathizes with their situation and does not
want to abandon them; they are not thereby excluded from the
life of the Church. Indeed, the Church wants them to practice
their faith. It is just that until their situation is resolved by the
competent ecclesiastical authority, they can no longer receive the
sacrament of Holy Communion — not as a punishment but as
a reflection of the fact that they are not really married in the eyes
of the Church.

To return to the sacrament of the Eucharist, they must have
recourse to the sacrament of Reconciliation and either resolve not
to engage in sexual relations or separate from their new "spouse,"
while also taking care not to cause scandal in their parish. If they
have children from this second relationship, separation may well
be an unattractive option. But since, objectively speaking, they
are not spouses, they cannot morally engage in those physically
intimate acts that are proper only to spouses.

If the man and woman inform you that their conscience told
them it was okay to receive Communion or that a priest told them
it was all right, you must gently but firmly let them know that
these answers, although common, are incorrect. Rather than con-
forming truth to our conscience, conscience must be conformed
to the truth, as noted in the Introduction. Many of these so-called
pastoral solutions do not really take seriously the idea that because
marriage is both an ecclesial and social reality, not simply a private
matter between the couple, an irregular marriage situation calls
for a solution that respects this truth as it attempts to bring heal-
ing to the relationship.

One final thought: It's possible that, for the sake of the children's good, the man and woman live together in the same home

but do not engage in sexual intercourse, and that the priest knows this. Judge not lest ye be judged (see Matthew 7:1-5; Luke 6:37-38, 41-42).

§§§

26.

What should you say to your primary-care physician when he recommends contraception or sterilization to you?

This can be one of those moments in life when we feel extremely embarrassed. Here we are lecturing our doctor about his supposed area of expertise! But we just may have to — especially in our day and age when contraception and sterilization are as common as tap water, and probably seen as morally uncomplicated as drinking the same tap water. But contraception is not only a technical and medical issue; it is also a moral one.

The Catholic Church's Tradition and Magisterium is firm and constant in teaching that the willing use of contraception is an *intrinsic evil*. This is not simply and only because of certain passages in Scripture (for example, the famous story of Onan in Genesis 38:8-10), doctrinally relevant though they may be. She also sees the immorality of contraception as another one of those moral truths of the natural law — that is, one we can know through our human reason.

There is no question as to *what* the Church teaches. This question, however, is not as much concerned with Church doctrine on contraception as it is with *what to say* to your doctor when he recommends that you use contraception — for example, that you go on the birth control pill.

We will assume that the doctor is not prescribing a contraceptive for health-related, non-contraceptive reasons, in which case it could be morally justified because although it would act as a form of indirect sterilization, your intention in using it would be to correct a health problem. It would then not be contraception per se. Rather, we will assume that the doctor is prescribing it for *contraceptive* purposes — that is, *to impede new life from coming to be*. We will also assume that your doctor is a Catholic, and that you have a good doctor-patient relationship with him or her.

A key component of your answer should involve showing your doctor the central moral difference between what the Church calls "periodic continence," or what is more popularly known as natural family planning (NFP), and contraception. Surprisingly, many in the medical field, doctors and nurses alike, have never heard of NFP; and if they have heard about it, they're not familiar with how it works. Moreover, many erroneously think NFP to be a "natural" form of contraception, just as the pill is an "artificial" form of contraception. Or they think it to be the old calendar-based rhythm method.

Well, is NFP a form of contraception, a way of immorally preventing a pregnancy? Many think so, including faithful Catholics, as I was made aware at a parish men's meeting that I attended. They reason that because the couple using contraception and the couple using NFP often have the same end in view — not to have a baby — they must be doing the same thing. But this is not correct. It must be emphasized that the NFP-practicing couple *does nothing to impede human life* — unless you count *not having sex* as preventing new life from coming to be.

I think that we don't grasp this point because we have largely lost sight of the significance of the individual human acts we perform: not only for our *doing* things (for example, realizing the goods of human existence) but for *determining* ourselves (for example, forming our moral character as good or bad). We become, in large measure, what we do. And what we become, in turn, disposes us to do certain things that reflect our already established good or bad character.

The NFP couple cannot become what they do not choose to do: that is, they cannot become contraceptors because they did nothing to contracept their individual acts of sexual intercourse. By contrast, we call the contracepting couples "contraceptors" precisely because that's exactly what they do — *contracept.* To put it another way: These couples *impede procreation*, rendering their sexual intercourse infertile — closed to the handing-on of new human life — by their own intentional action. That's why what they do is objectively immoral, while what the NFP couple does is not. (The Church speaks of good or just reasons for using NFP in order to avoid the contraceptive mentality.)

But there is another crucial reason why we fail to understand the moral difference between NFP (practiced for legitimate reasons) and contraception: We fail to *define* contraception accurately. To contracept, one has to do the following two actions: (1) freely choose to have sexual intercourse, and then one has to (2) do something to that sexual congress to block procreation. By the way, this is why a rape victim has the right to stop a rapist's sperm from reaching her ovum — thus possibly impregnating her — without violating the absolute norm against using contraception. Her act is an act of self-defense, not contraception.

So, as a faithful Catholic who is trying to live the Catholic moral life in all its fullness and beauty, you must respectfully tell your physician that you want no part of contraception (or direct sterilization, which is also objectively immoral). But you shouldn't stop there. You should also be prepared to inform your doctor how NFP radically differs from contraception in other significant ways, beginning with the fact that NFP, by helping a couple diagnose fertility problems, can assist a couple to *achieve* a pregnancy, something no contraceptive can do!

Moreover, there is also a large and growing body of literature and research showing that contraception is not only harmful to a woman's body (for example, as a cause of breast cancer), it is also harmful to the environment, especially by polluting the water supply because women on the pill excrete large amounts of leftover estrogen every day. (Two essays by Janet E. Smith provide excellent overviews of contraception's many negatives and NFP's many positives. The first, "Uncovering a String of Lies," appeared in *Our Sunday Visitor Newsweekly*; the second, "Green Sex vs.

Pink Viagra," appeared in the *National Catholic Register*, and these articles are available at their respective websites.) Given the facts, it is a scandal that the medical profession seems uninterested in promoting natural methods of avoiding pregnancy for licit reasons. But ignorance plays a role here as does, it must be said, the fact that there is no financial gain to be had with recommending NFP as opposed to contraceptives such as the pill, condoms, the patch, implants, IUDs, and so forth.

Yet when couples learn about the low rate of divorce among NFP couples, how NFP fosters spousal communication, is safe, very effective, and inexpensive, they want to know more. Some physicians will only stop prescribing contraception and transition to an NFP-only practice if their patients educate and persuade them. In a sense, then, you may have to "evangelize" your doctor and tell him why you reject contraception and embrace NFP. The reasons, as have been pointed out, are both moral and anthropological, as Pope John Paul II pointed out in *Familiaris Consortio* (n. 32).

§§§

27.

Is it morally bad to return a product that I have used?

Many of us, if we're honest with ourselves, have to admit that we have used a product or worn a piece of clothing knowing full well that we were going to return it after using it. Maybe we've even felt uneasy about doing so. I believe that this practice is morally wrong. The Golden Rule serves as a good moral criterion for showing why it's wrong: Would you yourself want to buy something that had been used before by someone else, even if only once or twice? I think that most of us would say no.

Moreover, by doing this, you are in effect using something that you have no intention of paying for. You're treating the item as a free rental, thus cheating the store — kind of like temporarily shoplifting the item.

Of course, this is different from the situation where you have no intention of returning something after you purchase it — you truly want to keep it — but nevertheless find yourself dissatisfied with it for one reason or another. You bring it back to the store and exchange it for a product that works, or doesn't have a defect, or clothing that fits. Your intention in these cases is not to deceive the store in any way. Nor need you feel you need to lie when the sales clerk asks why you're returning the item.

Sometimes people who buy with the intent to return after use accidently damage the product. They can then be tempted to lie and say they didn't cause the damage, and that they found it in that condition. Better to avoid the practice of the temporary shoplift entirely.

§§§

28.

In a democracy, is it really morally irresponsible for me not to vote, especially when the candidates don't agree with Catholic moral teaching?

It sure is irresponsible, especially in a democracy, where the fate of our country in so many areas lies in our own hands. One can make a good case for saying that citizens have not only a *right* to vote but also a *duty* to so. Many however retort: "But I'm only one vote, and that won't count for much!" But your vote *does* count. Sure, each voter is just that: an individual voter whose vote is counted only once. But when joined with like-minded citizens, voters can effect much good in the way of policy and programs by means of the legislators they elect and the kinds of laws that are passed by these representatives. To a large degree, we settle whether our country will be friendly to faith and the family or unfriendly by the kinds of people we elect to office.

But regardless of the impact of our vote, voting and political participation in general are ways in which we freely determine ourselves as individuals in our role as responsible citizens. As with the virtue of patriotism, voting has declined in our country. There are many reasons for this: apathy and cynicism are two. But in a democratic republican form of government, it is the citizenry that has the responsibility to change the system when it is not serving the common good, respecting basic human and civil rights, pursuing sound fiscal practices, and so on.

So much has been given to us by our country that, in a sense, as with God himself, we are in debt to her. With these blessings comes the obligation to shoulder the burdens of citizenship. In other words, we have a responsibility to serve our country by being good citizens, and that entails voting for those individuals who will maintain its goodness and greatness, as well as overcome its flaws.

Whether we are voting for city council representatives or mayors, senators or congressmen, or the president of the United States, we have to take voting seriously by educating ourselves about the issues of our day; in other words, we need to be *informed* voters. It's not enough to simply vote — indeed it can be harmful to do so — unless your vote is based on a familiarity with the issues and the candidates, not just their names and party affiliation. But our voting will be made all the more effective if we as citizens are *virtuous* citizens who do justice, respect others, help our neighbors, participate in civic affairs (including jury duty and the like), pay our taxes, and so on.

But what if I believe that there are no good candidates to vote for? What does citizenship entail then? Thus, for example, many Catholics will ask about whether they can vote for particular candidates who are pro-abortion but seem to advocate for programs that they claim are in accord with Catholic social teaching. Or, on the other hand, Catholics ask if they can vote for candidates who are pro-life but advocate economic policies that the voter thinks are contrary to Catholic social justice teaching. While recognizing that these two different types of candidates often hold many positions more or less in line with Catholic teaching on issues ranging from human life to foreign policy to the economy, when these types run against each other, the real question becomes: "Which candidate should I vote for?"

Catholics evaluating political candidates for office must first keep in mind that on many social issues — for example, gun control and affirmative action — there's room for a legitimate pluralism of views. There are the unchanging and always-binding moral principles of Catholic social doctrine, and then there are their prudential applications in political policies, programs, and platforms. Although some Catholic moral teachings involve absolute moral norms — for example, teachings on abortion and euthanasia — many issues pertaining to Catholic social teaching that deal with economic and political questions are at least open to reasonable differences of opinion and interpretation. This includes the question of war, and even capital punishment to some extent, however much Pope John Paul II severely restricted its use (see the encyclical *Evangelium Vitae*, n. 56; cf. CCC 2266-2267).

The life issues of abortion, euthanasia, embryonic and adult stem-cell research, marriage and family, and the like, therefore take on unique importance. As one author put it, abortion is not a "single issue"; it's a "singular issue." It's not that the other issues are unimportant; rather, it's that abortion is a privileged issue that takes on a certain priority and has a clarity and certainty that the other issues don't often have. The fundamental right to life is foundational for all of the other rights that the Catholic Church affirms, from education to health care to religious liberty. Without it, there can be no other rights.

So unless the pro-life politician is also, say, a racist or wants to harm the poor, a vote for the pro-abortion candidate could only be sanctioned in the rarest of circumstances, it seems to me. If all the candidates are anti-life and equally bad on economic issues as well, one may choose to not vote for any of them and write in the name of a friend who is pro-life. More, much more, could be said in response to the question.

Finally, the truth of all of the moral issues we have been discussing in this question can be known through the natural law, that source of non-revealed truth that is accessible to the human mind. So the Church's teaching on abortion, for example, is not only a matter of Catholic moral doctrine but also a matter of natural law and modern biological science. Other teachings, for example, that we are to take up our cross and follow Jesus (see Matthew 10:38), are known only through divine revelation or the teaching of the Church or her Tradition.

§§§

29.
What's so wrong about seeing a hypnotist or even consulting a fortune-teller or reading my horoscope?

Although the Catholic Church has, in fact, taught a great deal about the occult, I include this question simply because it is so commonly asked even by faithful Catholics. In addition, there are many people in our culture who think that these practices are harmless fun and have no moral dimension. The *Catechism of the Catholic Church*, however, includes these sorts of practices as those that are forbidden under the First Commandment ("You shall not have other gods beside me" Exodus 20:3), treating them in three paragraphs under the heading of "Divination and magic":

> **2115** God can reveal the future to his prophets or to other saints. Still, a sound Christian attitude consists in putting oneself confidently into the hands of Providence for whatever concerns the future, and giving up all unhealthy curiosity about it. Improvidence, however, can constitute a lack of responsibility.

> **2116** All forms of *divination* are to be rejected: recourse to Satan or demons, conjuring up the dead or other practices falsely supposed to "unveil" the future (cf. Deut 18:10; Jer 29:8). Consulting horoscopes, astrology, palm reading, interpretation of omens and lots, the phenomena of clairvoyance, and recourse to mediums all conceal a desire for power over time, history, and, in the last analysis, other human beings, as well as a wish to conciliate hidden powers. They contradict the honor, respect, and loving fear that we owe to God alone.

2117 All practices of magic or sorcery, by which one attempts to tame occult powers, so as to place them at one's service and have a supernatural power over others — even if this were for the sake of restoring their health — are gravely contrary to the virtue of religion. These practices are even more to be condemned when accompanied by the intention of harming someone, or when they have recourse to the intervention of demons. Wearing charms is also reprehensible. *Spiritism* often implies divination or magical practices; the Church for her part warns the faithful against it. Recourse to so-called traditional cures does not justify either the invocation of evil powers or the exploitation of another's credulity.

Although, as we noted, many people want simply to amuse themselves with such practices, these kinds of actions flirt with superstition, can give bad example, and can lead people to delve more deeply into such practices, with all the risks to their spiritual good that these entail.

But note that the *Catechism* doesn't say anything about *hypnotism*. Many people would argue that hypnotism, when having no connection with the occult and not done for a bad purpose, seems different. Many high schools, including Catholic ones, for example, have an all-night lock-in senior party. I'm aware that the party planners often hire a hypnotist who hypnotizes student volunteers to do various innocuous behaviors such as barking like a dog or walking around like a monkey.

Many might very well ask: "Isn't that an okay reason to allow hypnotism — just to have a little fun? And what about using hypnotism for medical purposes — for example, to help someone kick the smoking habit? What could be wrong with that?"

If hypnotism is used for genuinely *therapeutic* purposes, under trained supervision, then it can be both medically and morally sound. (Whether it works or not is another question.) This is why Catholic teaching does not condemn it as intrinsically evil. But to use it purely for entertainment purposes, where others are present, seems to me morally problematic.

My teenage children have been part of these high school hypnotism events, and although the hypnotism in these settings seems innocuous enough, there is always the danger, however minor, that, because someone's will is (or appears to be) weakened (however slightly), he or she could be led to do something bad, or that they could be led to do something or say something that would embarrass themselves or others. I don't want to sound too harsh in rejecting hypnotism for these occasions, but it's best to be on the safe side, than not. Better to rent a mechanical bull-riding machine! (But caution is called for!)

§§§

30.
Is it always wrong for me to violate copyright laws?

Just as we saw with questions six (revealing a house's flaws) and
eighteen (getting paid under the table), this one, too, is tangled
up with the law. And it can get extremely complicated. We won't
be able to deal with all of the nuances of the issue — we'll keep it
focused on the kinds of ordinary day-to-day questions that come
up. Two of the most common are: Can I photocopy an entire
chapter of a book without the publisher's permission? Can I reproduce ("burn") an entire music CD for myself or someone else
as long as I don't profit from it?

As our question is worded (Is it always wrong to violate copyright law?), the answer is that you cannot violate copyright laws,
at least in most cases. That would obviously be a crime. And so,
with a question of this type — similar to the question about paying under the table where legal rules are involved — it is morally obligatory for you to investigate the relevant law(s). This may
involve seeking out the advice of a knowledgeable person or an
expert familiar with the laws and regulations for that particular
issue. This is especially necessary where the law may be unusually
complex and filled with exceptions that may or may not apply in
your situation, as is the case with copyright. The website for the
United States Copyright Office is particularly helpful, and there
are books and other websites that will take you through current
copyright law and related matters.

On its website, the United States Copyright Office defines
copyright the following way:

> Copyright is a form of protection provided by the laws
> of the United States (title 17, *U.S. Code*) to the authors
> of "original works of authorship," including literary, dra-
> matic, musical, artistic, and certain other intellectual

works. This protection is available to both published and unpublished works.... It is illegal for anyone to violate any of the rights provided by the copyright law to the owner of copyright. These rights, however, are not unlimited in scope. Sections 107 through 122 of the 1976 Copyright Act establish limitations on these rights. In some cases, these limitations are specified exemptions from copyright liability. One major limitation is the doctrine of "fair use," which is given a statutory basis in section 107 of the 1976 Copyright Act. In other instances, the limitation takes the form of a "compulsory license" under which certain limited uses of copyrighted works [for example, sound recordings of musical compositions that are non-dramatic in nature] are permitted upon payment of specified royalties and compliance with statutory conditions. (http://www.copyright.gov/circs/circ01.pdf)

In the course of answering a question of whether scholars can republish the same material they've authored, Germain Grisez offers helpful moral advice — touching on such exceptions as "fair use" and "compulsory license" — when he argues this way:

Copyright law is complex.... Every academic has an obligation to try to understand it insofar as it applies to his or her teaching and research.... I cannot think of any use of material permitted by copyright law that would itself be unjust, although, of course, there are many ways of treating other scholars unfairly without violating any copyright. In general, there is a presumption in favor of obeying laws, and so in general copyright law should be obeyed. That one would not buy a particular book [for example, because it is too expensive] does not excuse making an unauthorized copy: doing so makes unauthorized, uncompensated use of another's property.

Grisez continues:

> In some cases, however, there can be a moral justifi-
> cation for making use of materials without the copyright
> holder's permission. For example, I think that copying
> for personal use out-of-print materials, including whole
> books needed for one's work, can sometimes meet the
> test of the Golden Rule and other relevant moral norms,
> as well as the legal principle of fair use.... Also, even if
> making a copy is not permitted by the principle of fair
> use, it sometimes really is reasonable to presume permis-
> sion, and then one can proceed without actually obtain-
> ing it. For example, if the textbook a professor adopts for
> a course fails to arrive on time, he or she might reasonably
> supply students with copies of a section to get the class
> under way, provided they will be required to purchase
> books when they arrive. Finally, the poor who need some
> copyrighted work but cannot obtain it without violating
> the copyright can be justified in doing so. (*The Way of the
> Lord Jesus*, http://www.twotlj.org/G-3-162.html)

This all seems quite sound to me.

Here's how the concept of fair use has been described on the
U.S. Copyright Office website:

> Section 107 [of Title 17, of the U.S. Copyright Law]
> contains a list of the various purposes for which the re-
> production of a particular work may be considered fair,
> such as criticism, comment, news reporting, teaching,
> scholarship, and research. Section 107 also sets out four
> factors to be considered in determining whether or not a
> particular use is fair:

1. The purpose and character of the use, including whether such use is of commercial nature or is for nonprofit educational purposes
2. The nature of the copyrighted work
3. The amount and substantiality of the portion used in relation to the copyrighted work as a whole
4. The effect of the use upon the potential market for, or value of, the copyrighted work

The distinction between fair use and infringement may be unclear and not easily defined. There is no specific number of words, lines, or notes that may safely be taken without permission. Acknowledging the source of the copyrighted material does not substitute for obtaining permission. (http://www.copyright.gov/fls/fl102.html)

Of course, works said to be in the public domain are not subject to copyright law and can be freely used by all. The University of North Carolina website has a helpful chart that offers useful information regarding when a work passes into the public domain.

As far as burning a CD goes or, as is probably more common today, Internet copying, the Recording Industry Association of America (RIAA), although not always promoting and protecting morally sound products (in other words, some of the artists and their music are morally offensive), has, in my opinion, a helpful list of "okays" listed under "the law" on its website. I reproduce that information in full here:

Internet Copying

o   It's okay to download music from sites authorized by the owners of the copyrighted music, whether or not such sites charge a fee.

o   Visit our list of Legal Music Sites or Music United for a list of a number [of] legal and safe sites where permission is granted and content is available for downloading.

o   It's never okay to download unauthorized music from pirate sites (web or FTP) or peer-to-peer systems. Examples of peer-to-peer systems making unauthorized music available for download include: Ares, BitTorrent, Gnutella, Limewire, and Morpheus.

o   It's never okay to make unauthorized copies of music available to others (that is, uploading music) on peer-to-peer systems.

Copying CDs

o   It's okay to copy music onto an analog cassette, but not for commercial purposes.

o   It's also okay to copy music onto special Audio CD-R's, mini-discs, and digital tapes (because royalties have been paid on them) — but, again, not for commercial purposes.

o   Beyond that, there's no legal "right" to copy the copyrighted music on a CD onto a CD-R. However, burning a copy of [a] CD onto a CD-R, or transferring a copy onto your computer hard drive or your portable music player, won't usually raise concerns so long as:

     o   The copy is made from an authorized original CD that you legitimately own.

     o   The copy is just for your personal use. It's not a personal use — in fact, it's illegal — to give away the copy or lend it to others for copying. [According to a 1997 U.S. federal law,

the No Electronic Theft Act, this would be
true even if there is no personal monetary
gain or commercial benefit involved.]

o The owners of copyrighted music have the right
to use protection technology to allow or prevent
copying.

o Remember, it's never okay to sell or make commercial use of a copy that you make. (http://
www.riaa.com/physicalpiracy.php?content_
selector=piracy_online_the_law)

Is there some gray area involved here? Yes, there is, in my
opinion, as a quick glance at any website dealing with this question will attest. But the argument that "everyone's doing it, so it's
okay and no big deal" doesn't quite pass muster, even if it has led
to a situation where, because so many are doing it, the little guy
is rarely prosecuted, with mostly the biggest offenders facing punishment. Technology has made it easy to download songs illegally,
but that does not make it right. Nor does the fact that recording
artists and other artists might be rich make it morally insignificant
to copy or download music and other files, say, movies, illegally.
To do so is to steal them.

With this question, as with many of the others, it is best to invoke the Golden Rule and the principle of fairness, as well as the
Seventh Commandment against stealing. The *Catechism* teaches
that this commandment

forbids *theft*, that is, usurping another's property against
the reasonable will of the owner. There is no theft if consent can be presumed or if refusal is contrary to reason
and the universal destination of goods. This is the case in
obvious and urgent necessity when the only way to provide for immediate, essential needs (food, shelter, cloth-

ing ...) is to put at one's disposal and use the property of others (cf. GS 69 § 1). (n. 2408)

Neither of these last two conditions would seem to hold in most cases with respect to downloading music, movies, and the like. That is, consent should not be presumed and refusal does not seem "contrary to reason." Thus, one would be hard-pressed to argue from "urgent necessity," however much one might desire a song or CD, although there may be a real need (as opposed to a desire) to do so with a (text)book, as we saw above.

Now, many, I'm sure, will disagree with my conclusion as being either too restrictive or impractical. But it's where my moral sense has led me. It will be interesting to see where you draw the line. After reading my answer to this question, you may decide to redraw it!

§§§

31.
Is it wrong for me to engage in "racial profiling" while going about my daily routine?

First, let's nail down what we mean by *racial profiling*. This has been a hot-button term and practice now for a good many years, made even more controversial by the U.S. Supreme Court's June 25, 2012, ruling on the contested Arizona immigration law. The high court upheld the so-called "show me your papers" part of the law but struck down other parts of it. In addition, the security measures brought into being after the terrorist attacks on September 11, 2001, also raised the issue of racial profiling to a prominent place in our national political conversation. The Trayvon Martin shooting death in February 2012 is another prominent incident of alleged racial profiling, in this case by an adult Hispanic male (George Zimmerman) of a black teenage boy. (Zimmerman was eventually acquitted.)

Our question is focused on the individual — rather than, say, on an institution such as the government or the police — making decisions based on skin color about people they interact with in their daily lives. And that, in fact, is the essence of racial profiling, despite the plethora of definitions for it.

In many ways, racial profiling can be morally justified when, for example, the police say that a white man was caught on camera assaulting another person in your apartment building and to keep an eye out for him. If the perpetrator of the crime was instead known to be white, then it stands to reason that "racial profiling" — that is, looking at suspects that are white instead of black or Asian — makes perfect sense and is reasonable, as well as morally justified.

In a real sense, if the perpetrator was known to be Asian or Hispanic, then we could also say that racial profiling — in the sense of watching out only for Asians or Hispanics that fit the description of the suspect — is not at all discriminatory either. We all "discriminate" in our daily lives against things that have the potential to harm us — for example, we don't allow convicted child molesters to teach in our schools — we rightly "discriminate" against them. The question becomes whether a particular act of discrimination constitutes an unjust infringement of another person's basic rights.

Both Church teaching and sound ethics see in *unjust* exercises of discrimination violations of human dignity and fundamental rights. Thus, to use racial profiling as a tool to single out individuals merely because they are of a particular race — apart from any reasonable basis or suspicion, or apart from any connection to the crime that their race may play in a specific situation (for example, in a hate crime) — is a serious trampling of another's civil rights. In a word, it would be *unjust*. (The same applies, by the way, to profiling someone on the basis of their religion.)

And so in daily life, the only kind of profiling that a person can engage in, racial or religious, needs to be rooted in some sound *reason* for the singling out, for the profiling. When there is no good reason present, then it is reasonable to suppose that racism or some other invidious prejudice may be involved. In other words, you are now profiling simply because you have it out for African-Americans, for example, and want to restrict their opportunities and rights, or unjustly accuse them of crimes.

People implicitly raise the question about profiling when they ask whether they can take race into account when thinking about moving into a new neighborhood or when walking down a street in a crime-ridden area after dark or when getting on an elevator alone in a rough neighborhood. Individuals need to be treated as individuals. The problem is *crime*, not the person's race. And so, we need to focus more on *behavior* than a person's skin color.

Nonetheless, as a matter of statistics and sociology, you can take race — whether black or white or other — *coupled with behavior* into account when evaluating certain situations that may pose a threat to you. If, for instance, the police say that middle-aged Asian men are robbing banks or individuals much more frequently in your community than any other segment of the population, you may ask: "Who is more likely to assault or rob me?" To show that this is not racist when applied to individuals of other races, we should point out that they can ask the same question: "Who is more likely in this situation to pose a threat to me?" — whites, blacks, and others included. The same is true of religion when the subject is terrorism. If Homeland Security informs us that radical Islamists are hijacking planes in disproportionate numbers to any other religion or group, we can profile those individuals meeting that description.

Our country was founded on the Declaration's principle that "all men are created equal." The Fourteenth Amendment speaks of how U.S. citizens are not to be denied "the equal protection of the laws." Therefore, any kind of racial profiling that would encroach on this affirmation of the equality of all — for example, by *presuming guilt* simply because someone is a certain color or religion (or by violating procedural safeguards to make sure that the innocent aren't harmed) — is not worthy of the principles of the American founding nor of the Christian view of the dignity of the human person. Safety and security are precious goods, but they need to be balanced with the rights that all individuals have by virtue of their God-given dignity. This is true whether they are U.S. citizens or not, but all the more so if they are U.S. citizens protected by the Constitution.

Admittedly, this is a difficult and sensitive question. Reasonable people will come to different conclusions. Mistakes will be made. Feelings can and will be hurt. Certain groups will be rightly or wrongly targeted and offended at times. Hence, all efforts must be made to avoid hatred and unjust discrimination in racial profiling, as well as to work with the groups most affected by the profiling. When that's not done, the racial profiling often becomes simply racism or religious persecution.

§§§

32.
Is it really all that wrong to go over the posted speed limit on the road?

The answer to this question may seem obvious: We are not to go above the posted speed limit — that's the law. As the *Catechism of the Catholic Church* teaches: "The virtue of temperance disposes us to *avoid every kind of excess*: the abuse of food, alcohol, tobacco, or medicine. Those incur grave guilt who, by drunkenness or a love of speed, endanger their own and others' safety on the road, at sea, or in the air" (n. 2290; emphasis in original). But note it doesn't specifically condemn *exceeding* the speed limit in every situation. Nor does the Vatican's 2007 document *Guidelines for the Pastoral Care of the Road*, specifically condemn it in absolute terms, simply quoting from a document that exhorts, "Road users should not drive too fast..." (n. 53). (Yes, the Vatican has a document on the rules for the road!)

Many drivers who go well over the speed limit say that it is not speed that kills but the fact that there's a slower driver in front of them (maybe one going well under the minimum posted speed). Or, they argue, correctly, that there are other known causes of accidents on the road. Some examples include: drivers who are distracted by texting or talking on the phone, by eating or drinking, or by children or pets; cars in various states of disrepair; road rage; poor driving skills; inexperienced teen drivers; and drivers who are impaired in some way, possibly from alcohol, drugs, or old age (on the latter problem, see question eleven). All true! But simply citing other abuses or problems doesn't absolve one from a moral wrong when one exists.

Usually, speeding is not a matter of distracted driving, although it very well could be. More often than not, people are speeding because they are in a hurry — they are late for work, for school, for appointments, and so on — or they are racing with other drivers. They speed, either intentionally or unintentionally, paying no attention to the speed limit. And they make no effort in the future to leave earlier so that they will not feel the urge to race wherever they're going.

Because the posted speed limit involves civil or criminal law, it should be obeyed unless there are extenuating circumstances where traveling over the speed limit is necessary to avoid injury or death, to protect life and health, and so on. Some concrete examples of these reasons could include the following: rushing a sick, injured, dying, or pregnant person to the hospital in an emergency; chasing after a kidnapper when the police are unable to respond in time for whatever reason; trying to get out of harm's way of another driver or a potential hazard; hastening to get to a sick or dying person; or keeping up with the flow of traffic on a busy, fast-moving highway. This list is not exhaustive, of course, but rather merely suggestive of why going over the speed limit may at times be justified.

Let me quickly add, however, that to avoid *reckless* speeding, we're talking about going a *reasonable* excess of speed in emergencies over what is posted. We're not talking of doing fifty mph in a school zone — or doing the same in a construction zone! That's *not* a form of cautious speeding. Rather, *cautious* speeding is the speed that a reasonable person who is similarly situated might think appropriate in these circumstances. Again, it's a good idea to apply the Golden Rule.

On this point, the virtue of *epicheia*, or equity, can be helpful. This virtue covers, it is said, those cases where justice can't seem to get the job done. There is something to be said for this virtue when the lawmaker writes the law — in this case, the speed limit — and foresees that there will be an imprecise and inconsistent keeping of it due to many factors, with drivers sometimes going well over it or drivers sometimes going well under it. And this imprecision is especially true with regard to speed limits: there is an "unwritten" rule (actually, a *custom* in most places) that the police will give you five mph over the posted speed limit before possibly ticketing you.

All of us can appreciate the value and necessity of speed limits and other road rules that exist to protect such basic goods as life, health, bodily integrity, and such instrumental goods as property, and so forth. But speed limits and other laws are not enough to safeguard these goods of the person. The moral virtues that we have spoken of so many times before in this book are also required. And they are many: prudence, justice, temperance or self-control, charity, and courtesy or neighborliness are prime among them for the obvious reasons. How many accidents would be avoided on our streets and freeways if people showed respect for other drivers and pedestrians, as well as respect for the rules of the road! This all presupposes that drivers have adequate knowledge of the Highway Code.

I will leave you with some wise words from the Vatican's *Guidelines for the Pastoral Care of the Road*: "The moral responsibility of road users, both drivers and pedestrians, derives from the obligation to respect the Fifth and Seventh Commandments: 'Thou shalt not kill' and 'Thou shalt not steal' " (n. 47).

P.S. The United States Department of Transportation website has information about state speed laws, aggressive driving and such. Some of you might find the site interesting and helpful.

§§§

33.

Can I rightly invest in companies that support immoral practices and products?

Catholics often contribute, knowingly or unknowingly, to the funding of immoral activity or products by the kinds of financial investments they make. The immoral activity that Catholics support through stocks or mutual funds includes not only matters of social justice but also issues running the gamut from pornography, homosexuality, and inhuman biotechnology research to the manufacture and promotion of cigarettes. There are a number of important questions to ask before investing.

First, is it appropriate to invest this money, or should I help others with it? That is, should I invest this money in order to provide for my future needs and those of my dependents, or should I donate it to help other people who are in need? Christians should think about investing not in the selfish ways of the world (see Matthew 6:19-20) but from the perspective that wealth entails the duty to use it fairly to meet genuine human needs, especially those needs that are most urgent.

Second, if I conclude that I should invest this money, I must ask what kind of investment will adequately meet the future needs that justify investing. A high rate of return is not the only criterion. I must ask, given my situation, what is a wise investment?

Third, I should ask myself how I can invest in ways that will likely promote genuine human goods, even at the sacrifice of part of the profit otherwise available.

Finally, I should consider not only the moral quality of the products or services of the companies I would like to invest in but also what Pope John Paul II called the *moral quality* of the business as "a *community of persons* who in various ways are endeavoring to satisfy their basic needs, and who form a particular group at the service of the whole of society" (encyclical *Centesimus Annus*, n. 35; emphasis in original).

The basic point of many of these questions can be summed up in one word: stewardship. We are to exercise economic stewardship even in the investment decisions we make.

The bottom line is this: We should not invest in companies that are engaged in intrinsically evil actions such as abortion or embryonic stem-cell research or even unfair labor practices. When it is a question of individual stocks, we have a choice regarding which ones we invest in. With mutual funds, however, we should use what is known as "morally responsible investment" — working with investment companies such as Ave Maria Mutual Funds that, in accord with Catholic teaching, screen out morally objectionable products and activities.

An essential element of the new evangelization preached by recent popes is the effort to go the extra moral mile and avoid as much as possible those entanglements in evil that are avoidable. Sometimes this requires greater effort, sometimes lesser. To knowingly and willingly invest in companies that are themselves known to support or promote businesses engaged in intrinsic evil — especially when you have an alternative — may very well constitute an unjustified "mediate material cooperation with evil."

§§§

34.

Can I keep money that exceeds the amount that I am actually owed at the store?

The short answer is no. "Well, what's the long answer?" you may be asking yourself. And that's a good question. Really, it is. But first the short answer. If, while at the store, I realize that the cashier has mistakenly given me back more money than I was owed, then I have a strict duty to return the change. If I don't, then I have broken the Seventh Commandment: "You shall not steal" (Exodus 20:15; Deuteronomy 5:19; Matthew 19:18). It's as simple as that. (The same is true if I am mistakenly in possession of store goods. I must return them immediately.)

The longer answer is: It depends. You're under no such obligation if it's the case that the amount of money is small and it would greatly burden you to return it (for example, you realize the overpayment later and would spend more money than is owed to buy gas to drive to the store and return the money). On the other hand, if it's a large sum of money, then you must make every effort to return it — if not immediately, then possibly the next time you shop at that store. You might even send a check to the store with a letter explaining exactly what happened. If you're concerned about appearing guilty of stealing the money — something that you did not do — you will have to either send cash or, if you can do so anonymously, send a money order.

The same goes for store and product discounts that are available to you if you are an employee at certain businesses. If you're not an employee, you're not to take advantage of the discount, even if the cashier says it's okay to say you are, as has happened to me in many stores.

§§§

35.
Is it morally blameless for me
to purchase luxury items?

Again, let me begin with a question: Why do you want to purchase this or that luxury good? What's your reason? Maybe you have a $75,000 sports car or an expensive boat on your always-wanted-to-have list. Or maybe you're interested in a $5,000 bottle of wine or an extravagantly expensive dinner. Now, there is nothing wrong with having nice things, especially if having those things is related to your vocation or work responsibilities — for example, if you are expected to entertain important clients in your home. But if having these high-priced goods is about nothing more than concern for status or supremacy, then those motives don't cut it, ethically speaking.

The virtues of justice and temperance come directly into focus when we deal with a question such as this — one not having a clear-cut moral norm prohibiting the purchase of such high-end stuff. Temperance comes into play because that's the virtue that moderates our desire for pleasure of all kinds, not just those associated with food, drink, sex, and even bad habits such as smoking. (Given what we now know about what grave harm smoking cigarettes does to one's health and others' health, I believe that people have a moral obligation in the stewardship over their body to refrain from the habit, stopping it if they have already started.) Justice is also very relevant because it helps us to give to others what is their due. For example, it makes me aware of how my spending decisions affect others economically, for good and for bad.

Responding to this question requires honest self-appraisal. It's true that in buying a luxury good, you might be stimulating the economy (something good), but are you neglecting to provide for your family's basic needs or help those who are less fortunate than you? In other words, could you put your money to use in more worthwhile and productive ways, such as donating it to the poor or even members of your own family who may need the money more than you need a sports car? That's something to think about.

To conclude: It's not intrinsically evil to buy or own such goods, but it may not be compatible with your personal vocation — that is, your special way of imitating Jesus in the world and sharing in his redemptive work — or the requirements of social justice. Figuring out when and if it's appropriate to buy such goods should be a matter of discernment, not simple desire. For many people, simplicity of lifestyle will be hard to abide in our consumerist culture. So, too, will it be difficult to overcome the "coveting" of goods that the Tenth Commandment condemns. But we must call to mind St. John's words: "If someone who has worldly means sees a brother in need and refuses him compassion, how can the love of God remain in him?" (1 John 3:17).

§§§

36.
Is there anything wrong with spending some
of my money buying lottery tickets?

No, unless you have a good reason not to buy them. Under its treatment of the Seventh Commandment, the *Catechism of the Catholic Church* teaches:

> *Games of chance* (card games, etc.) or wagers are not in themselves contrary to justice. They become morally unacceptable when they deprive someone of what is necessary to provide for his needs and those of others. The passion for gambling risks becoming an enslavement. Unfair wagers and cheating at games constitute grave matter, unless the damage inflicted is so slight that the one who suffers it cannot reasonably consider it significant. (n. 2413)

So there you have it. There's nothing intrinsically wrong with gambling in general or with buying lottery tickets in particular. But, as the *Catechism* expresses it so well, "The passion for gambling risks" enslaving the gambler. Our newspapers are littered with stories of people who have begun a life of crime, often resorting to embezzlement or robbery, in order to pay off gambling debts or who have simply lost everything — their marriage, house, job, car, and good reputation — to a gambling problem. It shouldn't surprise us. Gambling, like any activity that can bring us intense pleasure — whether it's eating, drinking, sex, or exercise — can become addictive. Then, overindulging in the activity can become immoral, although it may well be accompanied by various degrees of compulsivity and blame.

People must be very cautious and careful in their spending on lottery tickets. Are they prone to addiction? Is their personality type or family history a warning sign that they should not engage in any form of gambling, including that involved in lottery tickets? For most people, they can participate in games of chance and gambling without ever having a problem, without ever going into debt or neglecting their family obligations in favor of gambling — not to mention criminal activity. But even these folks need to ask themselves: "Would this money used in legalized gambling be put to better use in some other way or somewhere else?" "Am I not contributing with my money to the gambling culture which seems to affect the poor and lower class so much more harshly?"

Even though many argue that gambling can create jobs and generate large revenue for governments, one has to ask if it's all worth it — if, in fact, these claims are true (and that's disputed, though it's not our main focus). When we add up the increased level of crime associated with gambling and the human misery of gambling addiction, the resulting jobs and the additional tax revenue may not be worth the trade-off.

But if you want to buy a lottery ticket now and then — for amusement, to overcome boredom, for the thrill and hope of winning big, for the sake of water-cooler conversation, or as a gift — don't worry: you're not doing anything immoral. Just remember that your duty to pay the bills and meet your other financial obligations come first before you spend money on the lottery or on any other form of such entertainment — whether it be betting in a football pool at work or playing the slot machines in Vegas. The moral criterion that the *Catechism* provides is excellent: Our gambling will become morally bad when it deprives us of what is necessary to provide for our needs and those of others.

Is there a virtue or two needed here? There sure is! What did you expect by now? The two needed most are temperance and prudence; I'm sure that there are others. We have to control our urges to amuse ourselves, especially when there are serious reasons to have to control those urges, such as being out of a job and without a steady paycheck to buy the now-and-then lotto ticket. We also need to be prudent in how we spend our money, avoiding those things that we don't really need, trying to live within our means.

If I'm gambling, I also have to ask: "How will this activity affect my ability to stay debt free?" "How will it affect my ability to save money?" These questions bring us back to the concept of stewardship: "What kind of manager of my money am I? Do I squander it, or do I save and spend it wisely?" A last word, from Proverbs, seems appropriate here: "Precious treasure and oil are in the house of the wise, / but the fool consumes them" (21:20).

§§§

37.
How often and how much should I give to the Church and to charities?

There really is no set limit either in terms of a minimum or a maximum number of times that you should donate, nor is there a set amount that you should give when you open up your checkbook. We should be as generous as we can, as often as we can, while making sure that we are able to honor our financial obligations in whatever state of life God has called us to. We should not be giving away large sums of money to charitable groups or foundations if we are broke, bankrupt, or behind in paying the bills. The virtue of justice empowers us to give to others what is their due, thus respecting their rights. We violate justice when, for example, we don't give the proper amount that we are supposed to give or we give it to the wrong recipients or we give it at the wrong time.

You may have heard that there is a tradition in the Old and New Testament of *tithing* that some Christians, including Catholics, practice today. In his *Catholic Bible Dictionary*, the Catholic biblical scholar Scott Hahn defines a tithe as follows: "A religious offering consisting of a tenth part of one's harvest or income.... The tithe was paid to a sanctuary or directly to its ministers."

While the practice of tithing was obligatory for the Jews under the Old Law, the Catholic Church interprets the Sacred Scriptures as dispensing Christians from tithing under the New Law. But she also teaches that the Church's members must support the Church in some material fashion as their means allow. In this regard, the Church's Code of Canon Law stipulates, "The Christian faithful are obliged to assist with the needs of the Church so that the Church has what is necessary for divine worship, for the works of the apostolate and of charity, and for the decent support of ministers" (Canon 222.1).

The *Catholic Answers* website points to St. Paul's teaching about charitable giving as normative for members of the body of Christ:

- "On the first day of the week [Sunday] each of you should set aside ... whatever one can afford" (1 Corinthians 16:2).

- "So I thought it necessary to encourage the brothers to go on ahead to you and arrange in advance for your promised gift, so that in this way it might be ready as a bountiful gift and not as an exaction. Consider this: whoever sows sparingly will also reap sparingly, and whoever sows bountifully will also reap bountifully. Each must do as already determined, without sadness or compulsion, for God loves a cheerful giver. Moreover, God is able to make every grace abundant for you, so that in all things, always having all you need, you may have an abundance for every good work" (2 Corinthians 9:5-8).

Paul is saying that God wants us to give freely, from our hearts, not out of duty only but out of love. Many times when our financial situation does not permit us to give monetarily, we are able to volunteer our time and talents in ways that can support the Church and charities, whether building homes for Habitat for Humanity or working the parish festival. As Paul instructs, we give "whatever [we] can afford." Then, when our budget allows, we can support both Church and charity (including Catholic or non-Catholic charities) with our money. The important thing to remember is that we want to show love of God and neighbor through concrete action. We can manifest that love in diverse ways: giving treasure, time, and talent.

The virtue of prudence is called for in order to manage one's money wisely. Christians especially are called to a lifestyle that will enable them to contribute economically to the Church and to those less fortunate. This may well entail a life of simplicity that allows us to provide for our own basic needs but then also to meet the needs of the Church and the poor (see also question thirty-five). This simplicity will, of course, look different from individual to individual, from family to family, depending on many things, chief among them our personal vocations and our state of life. But Christians are called to shun the materialism and consumerism that is all around them in the secular culture.

Our personal vocation should be the chief standard or criterion by which we judge all that we do, including what we are to buy, sell, donate, retain, recycle, or repair. In this instance we must ask: "What ought I to give, and how often, in light of my personal vocation?" That is a question that each individual conscience will have to answer.

But to faithfully carry out our choices in the areas of our possessions, financial management, and charitable giving will require the virtues of moderation and fortitude, for obvious reasons: moderation, so that we are able to control our desires for creature comforts; fortitude, so that we have the resolve to stay the course with the decisions we have made, either to forgo a luxury, or even a need, in order to give alms to the poor and the parish.

The apostle Paul indicates in the text above that our sacrifice will be aided by God's never-failing grace: he will provide for all our needs and give us what we should sacrifice on behalf of others. Thus, there is also in play the theological virtue of hope, allowing us to trust in God's providence.

§§§

38.
What about giving to charitable organizations (for example, Susan G. Komen) that donate money to Planned Parenthood and other organizations involved in immoral activities?

Here's another question that touches on a very sensitive subject. It has similarities to question thirty-three. Many people donate to charities such as the United Way, March of Dimes, and Susan G. Komen for the Cure, for much of the good work that they do. Some even actively participate in their fund-raisers on the parish and local level (Komen's Race for the Cure is popular, for example). The problem arises when these organizations give a portion of their funds or grants to agencies that perform immoral acts, such as we find to be true with Planned Parenthood. To simplify things a bit, we will focus on Planned Parenthood and take as our charitable group Susan G. Komen, which fights breast cancer (Komen was formerly known as The Susan G. Komen Breast Cancer Foundation). The relevant principles involved can be applied to similar organizations and situations.

As you may know, in early 2012 there was heated controversy over funding involving these two groups, with Komen cutting off its funds to Planned Parenthood and then, under pressure, reversing its decision a few days later. Komen affiliates had been, they claimed, providing grants to Planned Parenthood for mammograms and clinical breast exams but then announced they were ending this support because of the congressional investigation into Planned Parenthood's alleged criminal activity in regard, for example, to facilitating underage prostitution. This investigation was initiated after the investigative pro-life group Live Action carried out an undercover "sting operation" of various Planned Parenthood clinics across the country. (Live Action generated its own controversy because some pro-lifers — I among them — argued that its undercover tactics involved lying. Others defended their actions by saying, among other things, that they did what all investigative journalists do in trying to expose wrongdoing: they told "falsehoods" to those who did not have "a right to the truth.")

Now, compared to Planned Parenthood's huge operating budget, including hundreds of millions in federal grants, the Komen funds were and remain small potatoes. But given Planned Parenthood's lucrative abortion business, Komen's affiliation with them was nevertheless very troubling — even if, as supporters argued, the monies weren't directly going to pay for abortions. Still, one could plausibly argue that the money Planned Parenthood didn't have to shell out for breast cancer exams could go toward providing abortion and contraception.

A full treatment of this question would involve our old friends, formal and material cooperation with evil. This traditional principle of moral theology is highly useful for sorting out the kinds of questions involved in whether participation in another person's evil-doing can be defended as morally upright. But the principle can get complicated, and I promised you, the reader, I would mostly try to avoid relying on it except for a few questions. I will simply say this, just in case you're curious: I believe that material rather than formal cooperation is involved when you, as a pro-life person, donate money to Komen and similar organizations. You intend only the *good* stuff that they do, not the bad. But here's the serious caveat: Just because an act is material rather than formal doesn't mean that it is morally good cooperation.

The question then becomes whether your cooperation is mediate (that is, not so direct and immediate), as well as remote or distant enough to justify the financial support. It may be justified, depending on whether there's a good or serious reason for this support — and, likewise, whether there's a similar reason *not* to give it — and as long as, in Komen's case, there's no alternative breast cancer organizations to give to. (But note: There is no moral imperative to donate to Komen in the first place.)

Additionally, you should determine if you are being unfair to the unborn (who are killed in abortion) in giving a donation to Komen and other groups who donate to Planned Parenthood. Here we are applying the Golden Rule again.

Lastly, however, one must avoid scandal. And that's a big question mark. Scandal here isn't just a minor matter of ruffling a few feathers. Rather, will my donation or participation be seen in any way as implying that I think a group's involvement with Planned Parenthood is a good thing, or that somehow the latter organization's abortions, not to mention its alleged encouragement of illicit activity, are not morally evil? Given all the dirty laundry (in addition to abortion) that's been revealed about Planned Parenthood in recent years, it may be a hard sell to show the opposite — at least to the satisfaction of our fellow pro-lifers.

So, where does this analysis leave us? Can I give money to Komen and similar non-profits or not?

One of the things that make dealing with this question so difficult — and which may serve as a very good reason for not donating — is that many of these groups have been vague, at least at times, about their support or advocacy of not only questionable organizations such as Planned Parenthood but also specific immoral practices such as embryonic stem-cell research. Often, you have to do quite a bit of digging on the Internet to find this kind of information. The question becomes more difficult still when we see that there is some difference in practices between the national organization and its local affiliates.

In the case specifically of Komen, if people in good conscience give money to the organization or participate in their fund-raising events, I don't think that they are guilty of doing something morally bad. I would strongly ask them, though, to reconsider the decision in light of the 2012 controversy with Planned Parenthood and the despicable nature of Planned Parenthood's business. And though it's one thing for an individual Catholic to donate money to Komen, for the Church to become involved on a larger institutional level (by sponsoring runs, for example) sends the wrong message, in my opinion. I do not doubt that this will cause grief and maybe even protest on the part of some who don't see what the big fuss is all about. (On a personal note, my own parish recently withdrew its support of Komen.)

But here is where the Church's pastors are called to remind all Catholics of the dignity of their baptismal vocation as adopted sons and daughters of God the Father. All Catholics in their own way are to do all they can to create a culture of life and thus defeat, or rather win over, the culture of death that Pope John Paul II spoke of in his 1993 encyclical *Evangelium Vitae* ("The Gospel of Life"). Although giving twenty-five dollars to Komen is not formal cooperation, and hence intrinsically evil, you should ask yourself: "In today's 'culture of death,' do I want to give to a charity that, despite the good works it might do, has decided to partner with the largest abortion provider in the country?" Might we need to answer that question by recognizing that we as Christians need to go the extra mile on behalf of our witness to the sanctity of human life and find other ways to defeat the scourge of breast cancer?

§§§

39.
Is it morally wrong to wish or pray for my own or someone else's death?

Let me turn to the New Testament to answer this question. In his letter to the Philippians, St. Paul gives what I think is the most succinct and searching treatment of the attitude that the Christian is called to have toward death (and life):

> My eager expectation and hope is that I shall not be put to shame in any way, but that with all boldness, now as always, Christ will be magnified in my body, whether by life or by death. For to me life is Christ, and death is gain. If I go on living in the flesh, that means fruitful labor for me. And I do not know which I shall choose. I am caught between the two. I long to depart this life and be with Christ, [for] that is far better. Yet that I remain [in] the flesh is more necessary for your benefit. And this I know with confidence, that I shall remain and continue in the service of all of you for your progress and joy in the faith, so that your boasting in Christ Jesus may abound on account of me when I come to you again. (1:20-26)

You may be young or you may be old. You may be beset with serious physical or mental infirmities that bring you pain and suffering and that lead you to pray for your own death. Or maybe it's a friend or family member who is suffering and you wonder: "Can I pray for this person's death?" Paul provides us with the right way to think and pray about this matter.

Paul seems to be saying in Philippians that he is already united to Christ while in his living body ("life is Christ"), but that dying will bring a closer union with Christ ("death is gain"). He also implies that whatever happens to him in the time he has left on earth, he will be faithful to his commitments, thus magnifying Christ in his body. He also knows that life in his physical body involves much good, and he is satisfied with that. But he tells us that he has another option: to be with Christ in heaven. And that presents him with a difficult choice! He truly longs to be with Jesus more than anything else. Yet in all honesty he admits that to remain in the body would be better for the good of the Philippians. With complete certitude, Paul knows that he will not leave them but instead continue his work among them for their growth in faith.

Paul's attitude must be our attitude. Many sick and dying or depressed individuals pray or wish for their death. That can be understandable — even natural. But wishing and intending are two different things. We often wish for things that are not in our best interest and that we would never act on, and rightly so. But Paul tells us that what we should desire is not death but Christ — even though death will be the gateway to eternal life, as it was for Jesus and is for all human beings.

The Christian Tradition and the Church's Magisterium have always taught that to intend one's own death (suicide) or the death of another (for example, through euthanasia) is intrinsically evil. It can never be morally sanctioned or good. Often, of course, mental illness can deprive the person of the awareness or freedom required to commit a mortal sin by these actions. Seeing one's own life, or the life of another, robbed of many mental and bodily functions can lead even people of strong faith to will their own or another's death. They think, erroneously, that they (or others) would be better off dead because they're either a burden or for other reasons, and so they pray for death to come.

While that approach is morally bad, a very different approach would be to pray for a good death, if death at that particular time is in God's plan for the person. We should pray that God's will be done always, whether in life or in death. To pray for a good death, however, means that we do not intend to kill ourselves or intend or wish that another die. Rather, it means that we die in such a way that our earthly trials and tribulations do not cause us to give up hope and lose faith or charity. It means that through our dying, we advance in the love of Christ.

All of us have to die at some time. Nothing is more certain. Death, although it is the "last enemy" (1 Corinthians 15:26) and a consequence of sin (see Romans 6:23; James 1:15), is natural in the sense that in our present fallen condition, we are destined to die. That doesn't make death something good or something that's easy to accept. But that we should die peacefully in the Lord, of natural causes, with our friends and family members surrounding us, is a true gift that we should embrace when it is our time. Here the attitude is very different from that of the suicidal person: in the face of inevitable death, after fighting the good fight against it, we are now resigned to see it as the next step or stage in our journey to meet Christ; there's no other way. Death, while it remains an evil (a privation of life), can now be *accepted*. (On his deathbed, St. Francis of Assisi uttered, "Welcome, Sister Death.") Accepting death, however, is vastly different from intending, or wishing or praying for death, or welcoming it as a friend.

Whatever be God's will for us in how and when we die, we pray that we have the courage and patience to accept the dying process that we must undergo. That may involve embracing some measure of suffering on behalf of Jesus — that is, redemptive suffering — joining it in hope and faith to his sufferings as atonement for sin: our own and that of others.

Pope John Paul II's 1984 apostolic letter *Salvifici Doloris* is a wonderful document on the Christian meaning of human suffering — one that I recommend you read and reflect on. It's available on the Vatican website. Indeed, both former popes, John Paul II and Benedict XVI, have been splendid models in our time for how to deal gracefully with illness, old age, suffering, and death.

§§§

40.
Am I allowed to knowingly accept a gift or donation that comes from a morally tainted source?

I would have to reply in the negative in most situations, unless certain criteria are met. Obviously, you must not have participated in any way in the immoral or illegal activity in the first place. But even if you played no part in the activity, taking a gift or donation from someone or some organization that has obtained this money or these goods by morally tainted means could give the impression (at least if others besides the donor are aware of the donation and its source) that such activity is morally legitimate. Here again, we face the issue of scandal. One must rule that out as a factor.

If the money was derived from serious crimes, such as drug trafficking or prostitution, you'd need to be even more careful about whether to accept it. There is, of course, the obvious danger of finding yourself indebted in some fashion to the donor for the ill-gotten gain that is now your gain — that is, the donor may possibly expect some sort of recompense or recognition for his contribution to you, especially if it is a large one. You would then be faced with the very real possibility of supporting the donor's criminal enterprise. This is why I would strongly encourage you to "pay back" the gift, informing the donor that you will not keep the gift for your own personal use, but that you'll be giving his original gift to a charity. Furthermore, you will make it clear that you will only take his donation this one time — possibly as a sign that you welcome what you see as the donor's possible small steps toward conversion. You don't have to let the charity of your choice know of the original source of your gift.

Since I presuppose in this question that the donor is, in most cases, a family member or friend, you then would also have an obligation to exhort the donor to abandon his criminal behavior and reform his life, especially if you had not done so with him in the past. I think that also would be another criterion for accepting the donation. This would be a way of showing that you care more about the conversion of the sinner than you do his money.

The virtue of prudence will be called for to help discern the proper response in this matter.

§§§

CONCLUSION

What We Have Learned

WE HAVE NOW EXPLORED many of the difficult questions of everyday ethics for everyday people — which all of us are — in everyday situations. There are obviously many other questions that we could have dealt with, but that would have made this book much longer — and more expensive! For instance, people ask how to handle the situation when they do not approve of their adult child's choice of a future spouse. Many also want to know about the morality of various enhancement operations such as breast implants and face-lifts and tummy tucks. Still others ask about how to avoid a heavy tax burden on their assets in a moral and legal way as they near the end of their life. There is even (and we see it in the Old Testament too) a moral dimension to what name to give your child, as the Jewish philosopher Leon Kass noted years ago when writing in *First Things* of how he would never name a son of his *Jack Kass*. Today, many baby names are either silly or just plain ridiculous. Germain Grisez deals with some of our questions (and many others), and deals with them in further detail in the work of his I cite several times in the text.

I have tried to provide answers that are informed by the moral virtues of prudence, justice, temperance, and fortitude, as well as, when relevant, the theological virtues of faith, hope, and love. I have also tried to avoid every form of legalism or an approach to the moral life that sees moral questions simply as a matter of the minimum I need to do to be good or to get to heaven. This common approach to morality sees moral norms as mere rules of the club that are subject to the whims of the lawgiver and the winds of change. Moreover, I have tried to steer clear of conventional morality; in fact, I have tried to challenge it when I thought it necessary. On the contrary, I have tried to root the responses of this book in moral truth, while at the same time recognizing that not every moral question is a matter of absolutes but admits of exceptions. In addition, I have also made every effort to explore both sides to a question when that was called for. Further, I hope that you have found some of my observations humorous.

You may not agree with every argument and point that I make in this book, but that's okay. On many of these questions (or at least aspects of them), there is room for the old adage "We can agree to disagree." More important, I hope that this book will help you grapple with these questions as well as others that you may encounter as you strive, with the help of the Holy Spirit, to live the moral life in Christ. It is, I believe, the most fulfilling and happy life that you will ever find.

For Further Reading

THE SECOND VOLUME OF Catholic moral theologian Germain Grisez' projected four-volume series, *The Way of the Lord Jesus*, titled *Living a Christian Life* (Quincy, IL: Franciscan Press, 1993), is devoted to answering two hundred difficult moral questions. This work is recommended for those who may be more advanced readers who are ready for a more technical treatment. It is available both online and in print.

A more accessible work, designed for a popular audience, is the late Msgr. William B. Smith's book, *Modern Moral Problems: Trustworthy Answers to Your Tough Questions*, edited by Father Donald Haggerty (San Francisco: Ignatius Press, 2012). The questions and answers in Msgr. Smith's book are divided according to topic areas: "Life and Death," "Sex and Marriage," "Fidelity and Dissent," "Justice and Social Order," and "Sacraments and Priesthood." The casuistry, or case-based reasoning, on display here is similar in approach to the one taken in our book.

Both of these works are fine supplements to *What's a Person to Do?* Although both authors treat a few of the questions taken up here, at least in some form or another, the book you presently have in your hands is largely dealing with questions not included by them.

Finally, Our Sunday Visitor publishes, bimonthly, *The Catholic Answer,* which often treats difficult moral questions in a question-and-answer format. It is also available online at http://www.osv.com/TheCatholicAnswer/tabid/7629/Default.aspx.